More Praise for *Social Media at Work*

"All business leaders need to be aware that social media technologies have the capacity to fundamentally reshape the way work gets done and sustainable advantage is obtained. This book shines a bright light on leading practices and provides wonderful insights into developing your own approach."

—Alan Matcham, associate, Management Innovation Laboratory, London Business School

"This book provides fresh ideas about the critical role that social media play in winning organizations."

—Mike Duffy, dean, School of Business and Professional Studies, University of San Francisco

"If you ever thought social media was just for teens or was a workplace time-waster, think again. *Social Media at Work* makes the business case for using social networking in the organization."

—Fred Johnson, president and CEO, Credit Union Executives Society

"Offers leaders clarity on using a powerful toolbox to better attract, retain, and develop business talent."

—Edward E. Gordon, author, *Winning the Global Talent Showdown*

"Socialization in the workplace now has a guidebook for furthering skills and advancing careers. Jue, Alcalde Marr, and Kassotakis truly drive it home."

—Peter Amato, CEO, Inner Harmony Group

"*Social Media at Work* is immensely helpful in showing uses of social media in organizations today. The ideas about leveraging large networks of connections for co-creation and mass collaboration are useful to build relationships among contributors of any large project."

—Charles Wankel, Ph.D., associate professor of management, St. John's University

"Engagement and performance are now to be attained through social media, networking, and strategy. This book is a wake up call for corporate leaders who want to survive in a fast-changing and complex world. Enlightening, simple, concrete. A guide for action."

—Dr. J. Robert Ouimet, chairman and CEO, Holding O.C.B., Inc., Cordon Bleu International, and Ouimet Tomasso, Inc.

"People at their core are social beings and we have now become a media-immersed, electronically-connected society. Anyone interested in using the latest communications 'gizmos' will enjoy this book."

—Jon M. Corey, Ph.D., vice president, NEXTCARE, Urgent Care Corp

"A must-read for CEOs, entrepreneurs, managers, and human resource executives. If you deal with Gen Yers or Gen Xers and you want to grow and compete internationally, reading this book will help you become effective, innovative, and successful."

—Dr. Prasad Kaipa, executive director, Center for Leadership, Innovation and Change, Indian School of Business

"Jue, Alcalde Marr, and Kassotakis have hit this one out of the park. Emotional intelligence in business is the wheel, and social networking is the grease. *Social Media at Work* gets this loud and clear."

—Esther M. Orioli, author, *EQ Map*, and chief architect, 21DayClub.com

"A comprehensive review of the changing landscape of today's social media world and a must-read for senior executives who want to challenge and retain the next generations of business talent."

—John W. Lohre, vice president, Wealth Management, Securant Bank and Trust

"Once you start reading this book you'll be totally absorbed—it is rich and practical. I recommend it to managers and leaders who are looking for new and innovative approaches to improve employee performance."

—Robert C. Preziosi, professor and faculty chair of HRM, H. Wayne Huizenga School of Business and Entrepreneurship, Nova Southeastern University

"At last a book that takes the mystery out of social networking within organizations. *Social Media at Work* provides a valuable road map of how to tap the resources of a company's heart and soul. Filled with insights and examples, this book is essential reading for anyone who wishes to lead in a post modern world."

—Ernest D. Chu, author, *Soul Currency*

"With practical stories from every sector, this book will shift your thinking radically to the possibilities of social media. It's an engaging resource to accelerate your strategic paths to success."

—Shelly Wilsey, director, International Leadership Association

"*Social Media at Work* provides a solid case for why your organization needs to embrace this global phenomenon. All of us can create more connected, innovative, and agile organizations using social media."

—Ginny Von der Schmidt, chair, The Institute for Management Studies, San Francisco

"Successful executives are driving toward increasingly loftier goals. This powerful book highlights how social networking tools can help make those goals into a reality, especially during uncertain times."

—Dr. Ronald Lesniak, CEO, Teledex LLC

"*Social Media at Work* is one of the de facto standards that the talent development community will use to reinvent their industry."

—Scott Saslow, founder and executive director, The Institute of Executive Development

SOCIAL MEDIA AT WORK

SOCIAL MEDIA AT WORK

How Networking Tools Propel Organizational Performance

Arthur L. Jue
Jackie Alcalde Marr
Mary Ellen Kassotakis

JOSSEY-BASS
A Wiley Imprint
www.josseybass.com

Published by Jossey-Bass
A Wiley Imprint
989 Market Street, San Francisco, CA 94103-1741—www.josseybass.com

Jossey-Bass books and products are available through most bookstores. To contact Jossey-Bass directly call our Customer Care Department within the U.S. at 800-956-7739, outside the U.S. at 317-572-3986, or fax 317-572-4002.

Jossey-Bass also publishes its books in a variety of electronic formats. Some content that appears in print may not be available in electronic books.

Library of Congress Cataloging-in-Publication Data

Jue, Arthur L., 1966-
  Social media at work : how networking tools propel organizational performance / Arthur L. Jue, Jackie Alcalde Marr, Mary Ellen Kassotakis.
      p. cm.
  Includes index.
  ISBN 978-0-470-40543-7 (hardback)
1. Social media. 2. Social networks. 3. Organization. I. Marr, Jackie Alcalde, 1962- II. Kassotakis, Mary Ellen, 1953- III. Title.
HM742.J84 2009
303.48'33 —dc22
                        2009029078
Printed in the United States of America
FIRST EDITION

HB Printing   10 9 8 7 6 5 4 3 2 1

Contents

*To trailblazers everywhere—the groundbreakers,
innovators, pathfinders, and pioneers—who courageously
push the social media envelope*

SOCIAL MEDIA AT WORK

1

SOCIAL MEDIA AT WORK

On Saturday morning, August 23, 2008, at 2:45 in the morning, cell phones across the globe were buzzing with the text message announcing Joe Biden as the Democratic vice presidential candidate. Throughout the weekend, those who received the text message talked in restaurants and community meetings to discuss the implications. As the media spread the story, the unique way the announcement was revealed became almost as important as the choice of running mate.

The 2008 U.S. presidential election was unprecedented in many ways, one of which was the wave of support from younger Americans who seemed to be suddenly awakened to the political landscape. The swell of energy, passion, and commitment from such a wide variety of voters, particularly younger ones, swayed the polls in favor of the Democrats. The use of social media was a key factor in generating that energy and mobilizing a large community to achieve the common goal: elect Barack Obama. Regardless of his or her political beliefs or organizational affiliation, any community activist, corporate leader, or entrepreneur would love to create and harness that kind of fervor. Imagine what could happen if this were applied at work.

If you are part of an organization—profit, nonprofit, big, small, community, corporate—working with others to achieve common goals is the name of the game. Organizations of all kinds want to engage employees, clients, customers, suppliers, and partners, building brand loyalty to their products and services.

But in today's world, leaders face an increasingly difficult environment in which to accomplish these goals. Ever accelerating rates of change are the hallmark of our postmodern society. Economic uncertainty, shorter development cycles, flatter organizational structures, and transforming social institutions are all coevolving at a pace never before experienced. Executing with speed and excellence has become a sacred mantra of corporate survival if leaders are to keep stride with increasingly fierce global competition.[1]

If leaders are committed to gaining and sustaining competitive advantage, they will need to rely on engaged and committed employees and partners. In this volatile environment, the emerging phenomenon of social media can create an extraordinary opportunity for savvy leaders and organizations to achieve this advantage. These tools are accelerating and enhancing employee innovation, engagement, and performance. Those who are actively using social media in their organizations can be confident that they have new ways to improve their business performance, create long-term capability, and ultimately sustain their success.

Leaders everywhere should seize the opportunity to incorporate social media into their organizations to improve performance and to build highly energized teams and positive cultures. The advantages also include increased organizational learning, enhanced change readiness, and stronger relationships. As leaders learn to leverage social media *inside* their organizations just as individuals do *outside* their organizations, a tremendous boost of agility and vitality is unleashed. Within organizations, social media demonstrates the new reality—the reality that employees are cocreators of organizational success rather than servants of the company who simply salute and take orders.

The leaders we have talked with believe that social media helps them extend their personal leadership influence in uncertain times by accelerating employee development, improving succession planning, and attracting energized pools of new workers in the war for talent. It is a powerful means of continually revitalizing the spirit, heart, and soul of the enterprise. Ultimately, individuals, groups, and organizations will be able to reduce the time it takes to make decisions. This new speed will impact performance and will improve organizational and social innovation.

Why "Social Media"?

In recent years the popularity of social media has spread like wildfire. Yet just as a wildfire can evoke panic with its random and chaotic movement, the ripple effects of this technology are catching many organizational leaders by surprise. If you're among those feeling the anxiety and anticipation about how this proliferation of social media will impact your organization, we can certainly empathize. We have felt the same sense of urgency about understanding and tapping the power of social media in our professional activities.

A short year ago, we were in heated discussion about how to improve our talent management services at Oracle. How can we engage our leaders more? How can we extend our learning process over time? How can we create communities to exchange wisdom and experience? There was a sense of urgency among the team of leaders in the Global Organization and Talent Development group. We knew that our leaders were constantly looking for ways to stay ahead in the marketplace. And we knew that a large percentage of our employees were expecting us to deliver solutions that enabled them to work and learn in ways with which they were most comfortable—online. We were aware that social media offered us a new set of tools to accomplish this, and became energized when we challenged our assumptions about how to enable people to participate in the talent management process. We were convinced that the use of social media would encourage more involvement and better outcomes. But some concerns came out as well: Once we invite participation, how do we guide the effort so that it is most productive? How do we combat organizational fears? How do we engage those leaders who may be skeptical about changing their behaviors? At the end of the meeting, someone said, "I bet a lot of other people are wrestling with these same questions; we should write this all down to share with others."

If you're reading this book, you know there is a game-changing shift happening, and you are grappling with the very same questions we were. You know you should do something . . . now. We based this book on our own experiences confronting the wave of social media in the workplace and wondering how to make sense of it all.

The Changing Landscape

The term *social media* typically refers to the many relatively inexpensive and widely accessible electronic tools that enable anyone to publish and access information, collaborate on a common effort, or build relationships. This may sound like the "same old thing," but it's the advance in technology and the changing behavioral norms that have brought a whole new meaning to these activities, supercharging the volume of exchanges among people and extending their reach to every corner of the globe.

When we chose the definition of social media that best describes the focus of this book, we gravitated to the most simple and profound one, given to us by Richard Dennison, senior manager of social media at British Telecom: "Social media is about *participation*." That participation can take the form of simply viewing relevant information that was previously hidden from view. But most often it takes the form of communicating, collaborating, and connecting with anyone, anywhere, anytime.

It's about the *interactions* between people—individuals and groups—and the great potential to share more, learn more, and accomplish more than our grandparents could ever dream possible. Unlike traditional forms of media, which have limited pages or time on the airwaves, social media is "infinite" in its potential.

Social media is represented in various forms and functions: discussion forums, blogs, wikis, and podcasts, and may include the use of videos and pictures. Each of these tools uses a special kind of *social technology* (a communication platform that makes connections possible) called *Web 2.0*. Web 2.0 is the phase of the Internet that enables anyone to create information online. You're likely to have already used some of the popular tools, such as Facebook and LinkedIn, for social networking, Flickr and Snapfish for sharing photos, Wikipedia and Wikispaces for collaborating to share knowledge, and Blogger.com or Wordpress for sharing ideas through blogs. These are just some of the social media gaining momentum through viral marketing at the time of this writing.

The social media wildfire rages on, fed by the high winds of at least three converging forces: the nature of the business environment, changing workforce demographics, and rapid advancements in software technology that enable social connection. Although we will be exploring these forces in more detail in Chapter Two, let's take a quick look at them now.

The Changing Business Environment

The constant flow of information made possible by the Internet has created a more complex business environment—more information, more technology, more possibilities for partnering, more unprecedented challenges. In addition, many organizations operate in multiple countries, and employees have become accustomed to working with colleagues across the globe. Because information is available to anyone, the ability to use it in new ways has become a hallmark of the current business landscape.

We have moved from the industrial era well into the information age. Employees who are able to synthesize new information, advance research, and create new innovations are highly valued. E-commerce has changed the way we purchase goods. Trade and consumption are shifting as well. The "long tail" theory, first described by Chris Anderson in a 2004 *Wired* magazine article, shows how marketing and production strategies are changing; that is, companies are counting on selling a smaller volume of unique items to a wider variety of consumers over a long period of time. This theory has been applied to alternative workforces as well. For example, the work that used to be performed by employees or outsourced to contractors may now be given to an undefined larger community that will contribute via the Internet, leveraging the concept of mass collaboration.[2] This is one of the many ways businesses are rethinking how they use their human resources. Traditional ideas of the "typical" career life cycle are becoming obsolete.

Changing Demographics

As the world turns, our global population distribution is shifting. With each successive generation, people are becoming increasingly comfortable working with Internet tools, which dramatically change the nature of work, whether the user is in a nonprofit organization or a commercial business, whether he is a line employee or a senior executive. Gen Yers, or Millennials, are generally extremely comfortable with communicating, connecting, and collaborating via social media. In fact, they demand that their companies provide this capability. The Obama campaign understood this opportunity to reach the younger voters where they "lived" through social media. Many Traditionalists, Baby Boomers, and even Gen Xers are still unfamiliar with this way of working and living. We will discuss how leaders struggling to use social media tools to recruit, retain, and develop their workforces need to remember that one size does not fit all.

Software That Enables Social Connection

Traditional media—newspapers, television, and radio—have been effective means of communications. But with the advent of newer technologies, other forms of communication are proliferating at great speed. The Internet has forever changed the way we communicate. Newspapers have gone online, television news programs are now available on the Web, prime-time shows are available for replay on network Web sites, and radio programs are now available to download and play on mobile devices. Of course, the Internet has also given rise to social media aimed at enabling relationships and collaboration. The speed of this proliferation is rather unprecedented.

Various reports show that year over year, the use of global social media tools has increased fourfold and greater. Various types of social media are everywhere. We can't escape them. A revolution is under way. Organizations may choose to ignore this phenomenon at their peril—or they can actively choose to incorporate social media into their regular operations. Doing so may be uncomfortable for many leaders who fear that communicating through social media can take on a life of its own. They may not recognize the value of employees' engaging in a constant exchange of ideas. However, we believe that these cautious leaders will soon see that employee use of social media will prove more advantageous to the organization by harnessing information that can be transformed into knowledge and innovation.

Short-Term and Long-Term Benefits

All organizations want to meet their annual goals, but they also want to maintain their success long into the future. To do both, they must focus on key business levers for short-term performance (such as cost and operational efficiency) as well as longer-term capability (such as talent management and employee engagement).

Speed and innovation continue to be competitive advantages in every field. Social media can enable organizations to bring innovations to light and fruition much faster. In an interconnected and distributed world, there are more "sensors" to monitor activities and opinions. Experts across the globe can track progress in a 24/7 environment, enabling diverse constituents to perform as one unified team across time and space. Furthermore, the information can also be used to capture real-time feedback on a product, service, or strategy, enabling adjustments to be made in a quick-fire fashion.

An organization can foster innovation by bringing ideas to the surface throughout its departments and functions. Previously, employees who were not close to a project may not have been aware that they could contribute to the effort. Social media tools such as forums, social networking profiles, and wikis enable these individuals to offer their ideas and experiences when the project team signals the need for assistance. Groups with like interests can quickly emerge and then disband when no longer needed. And collaboration can include groups who were previously left out. The use of various social media can help companies include external partners and customers in creating new business opportunities.

Many organizations are already taking advantage of social media to boost short-term performance. Throughout the book and especially in Chapters Four and Five, we'll share examples of how Cisco, BT, Humana, Intel, and other companies are using social media strategies that enable employees (and even company alumni and retirees) to communicate more effectively, access needed information faster, and collaborate with a wider network across the globe. But perhaps less visible are the ways social media helps build an organization's long-term capability, an attribute that relies heavily on attracting and keeping the best employees. In the quest for securing the interest of stellar job candidates, some organizations are using social media for employee recruitment, promoting the company's values, strategies, and challenges to a targeted audience. With the continuing increase of mergers and acquisitions across the globe, social media can also play a key role in speeding up the integration and adoption of corporate cultures and values, and serve as a bridge that spans cultures, fostering acknowledgment and understanding of diverse populations, beliefs, practices, products, and services.

Indeed, social media is helping transform the entire domain of human relationships. Employees can reside anywhere as they initiate projects, form teams, and produce outcomes. Given this new world of work in the twenty-first century, organizations can increase the value of their knowledge and improve their chance of thriving for years to come by deciding to support, design, and cocreate formal social media strategies.

Achieving Adoption in Your Organization

Although the business benefits of social media are significant, many organizational leaders and corporate executives are ill prepared to harness it strategically. Our aim in this book is not only to introduce the richness and variety of social media but also to offer insights and advice derived from the experiences of many organizations. When haphazardly implemented, change can inhibit productivity and employee commitment. So we will likewise offer suggestions about how to accelerate time-to-value and avoid unnecessary delay in establishing programs enabled by social media.

At its core, use of social media depends on human nature and taps into both the energies and frailties of human emotions. A disruption in the status quo is threatening for most, particularly if the processes, tools, and relationships involved will change. Just as when crossing into any new frontier, implementing and adopting social media are rife with unforeseen challenges, but the risks are counterbalanced by the promise of success. In Chapter Six we offer a recommended approach and useful tips for successfully gaining adoption. Even without a thoughtful and purposeful approach to implementation, most organizations will still experience some value from social media. Many employees already communicate, collaborate, and connect in their personal lives, and those relationships are benefiting the organization, as employees are more equipped to share their knowledge and resource networks. With just a little more thought and insight, you can multiply the benefits many times over.

Of course, every organization is different, and the potential application of diverse social media can vary greatly. But the playbook we present in Chapter Six offers a basic framework for creating social networks that can help organizations capture the greatest advantages of real-time collaboration. Processes can be redesigned or reconfigured more quickly, and organizations can reap the rewards.

Join the Conversation

If you are still asking yourself why you or your organization need to pay attention to social media, consider the following: in a world of viral communications and relentless change and evolution (or perhaps revolution!), it is more imperative than ever before to furnish employees and teams with the tools to connect, create new connections, and stay connected. The ability to share information more quickly can lead to better decisions and more commitment from those people who contribute to the discussions or who simply read and stay abreast of the issues presented. Employees, as well as customers and clients, quickly become experts on products and services. Through the formation of affinity groups, your customers, peers, clients, suppliers, and employees can become your strongest allies, especially when they are part of the cocreation of your products and services. Social media can help you form a close connection with a broader pool of ideas. Every executive will need to incorporate social media into his or her organization's daily operation. To work in the new millennium otherwise is like "stopping the clock to save time." It just won't be possible. As we'll discuss further in the book, capitalizing on social media can also help in the process of creating sustainable competitive advantage.

Establishing a successful organizational social media strategy is challenging, but leaders who don't attempt it will be left behind as others try, learn, and try again. We are convinced that the courageous will inevitably be rewarded with greater organizational health, improved business performance, and long-term sustainability.

We hope this book will provide a basic overview of social media to help in understanding the most prevalent tools available. But we've found that it is one thing to understand the various forms of social media at an intellectual level and quite another to figure out how they fit into the structure of daily professional interactions. To ease the confusion, we provide a simple road map for how to grasp, integrate, and leverage the many uses of social media in organizations and communities of practice. Most important, we include examples of those who may be a few steps ahead of the curve in implementing and learning how to take advantage of social media in their organizations.

The leaders we've interviewed openly shared their experiences of how they are implementing social media at work. These forward-thinking leaders and organizations are blazing the trail right along with you. They want you to join the conversation as well, to expand everyone's wisdom. At the end of each chapter, you will see opportunities to share your questions and ideas on our social networking site.

Whether you are a manager struggling to tap the collective knowledge of your virtual team members or an executive attempting to foster greater collaboration in your business decisions, we hope that the stories and examples we've included will resonate with you. If you're an organization development practitioner diagnosing culture or a human resources leader working on succession planning or growing the leadership pipeline, we are confident that social media can help. It has certainly helped us. Virtually any leader can find ways to improve performance or cohesion among team members through social media. The Obama campaign did. We anticipate that you will too.

2

THE CHANGING LANDSCAPE AND WHAT IT MEANS TO YOU

The sun poured in through the huge window and heated David Woodbury's headquarters office in Kentucky; outside, the treetops were bending with an insistent wind, and in the distance, black clouds threatened a thundershower. But Woodbury was oblivious to the changing weather that afternoon. He was too immersed in his planning. He scratched his pen feverishly on his notepad, eager to capture the flood of ideas that resulted from the meeting he just held with Humana's chief human resources officer, Bonnie Hathcock.

As the director of succession management, Woodbury is responsible for ensuring the readiness of the next wave of leaders that will sustain Humana's success. Although he may not have noticed the changes in Louisville's weather that day, his energizing meeting was a result of assessing the changing environment outside and inside Humana's eighteen-thousand-employee organization. As a health care benefits insurance company, Humana is facing the increasingly challenging dilemmas of rising health care costs and inconsistent levels of care for its customers. The company must be capable of developing new and valuable services in order to accommodate a growing variety of customers. Currently Humana has business units that serve audiences beyond its staples of group medical and dental insurance plans. These business units include military health care, individual medical and dental, venture capital investing, and the Medicare-eligible population. Humana's ability to create innovative and affordable solutions for these diverse audiences is key to its success.

Woodbury and Hathcock were also well aware of the challenges they face in identifying strong successors for the company's executive leaders. Like human resources managers in many other organizations, they anticipated the impact of losing their senior leaders as many retire after several years of dedicated service. When these leaders leave, they take with them their Humana awards, photos of colleagues, and cherished memories of their careers—as well as their years of experience, knowledge of company history, and hard-earned wisdom born of setbacks and successes. The foundation of Humana's workforce is shifting as the company hires new, younger employees. Many of the middle managers are still developing critical skills and gaining the experience needed to lead large organizations.

As home to the sports world's most famous two minutes, the Kentucky Derby, Louisville is steeped in tradition and the community ties of longtime residents. Humana reflects this strong value of relationship building; connections between people have become increasingly important, and networking is woven into the fabric of the company. An employee's professional network can play a significant role in helping him get work done as well as in shaping his career. But with the increase in younger new hires, many employees have not yet built a community of resources, and many senior leaders are not yet aware of where the talent and potential resides in the organization.

Woodbury and Hathcock had been discussing these issues for quite some time, and Hathcock felt the need to get in front of this wave. So that afternoon she challenged Woodbury with two new top priorities: enabling Humana employees to find the best ideas to meet their immediate needs, and enabling the company's executives to identify the leadership talent needed for long-term success.

The essentials of the plan filled Woodbury's page: foster the information exchange between newer and more tenured employees, support creativity and innovation, show senior leaders the value derived from greater collaboration among employees, improve the process of selecting key talent, capitalize on the strong culture of relationships and networking, play to the younger employees' comfort with social media tools, build on our existing database of leader profiles, and create a social networking platform to enable all employees to tap the skills of their colleagues more quickly.

Humana had a good head start. For succession planning, the company had already created online profiles of employees to use in the performance review process. These profiles encouraged a rich conversation that included each employee's career aspirations and the appropriate specific development plan. However, Woodbury and Hathcock recognized the power to be gained if employees were able to view each other's profiles and search on particular expertise. So Woodbury's primary effort was to establish an internal social networking site, similar to Facebook or LinkedIn, with a strong built-in search mechanism. In addition, Woodbury envisioned employees having their own blogs to spread expertise, commentary, and provocative ideas to stimulate innovation.

As an outcome of this vision, Humana is currently experimenting with social network analysis software to identify communication patterns and the people who are nodes of influence and hubs of information exchange. Woodbury and Hathcock believe that it may be possible to replicate the best practices of these "ultracommunicators" and purposefully use the organization's natural communication pathways to share information more efficiently.

TRAILBLAZER

Another way in which Humana uses social media is through technology-enabled online simulations. With this software, participants interact in new ways by creating "what if" scenarios and discussing the business impact of various decisions. The company began using these simulations with its leadership teams to promote a shared view of its complex business model and the relationships among health care providers, brokers, consumers, and the organization. The company will expand this systemic view by including a variety of stakeholders in the simulation experience. Hospitals, government agencies, and consumer representatives will work together to model different ways to bring health care solutions to fruition. The strategy to engage its workforce and its consumer base is a well thought out way for Humana to improve health and wellness among its many consumer populations.

Humana also believes in an engaged and healthy workforce and sees its employees as maintaining balanced work and home lives. But Woodbury recognizes some of the challenges presented by social networking technology and, more important, by the policies the company may create to provide boundaries. Says Woodbury, "We like to say 'bring your whole self to work,' but sometimes we really don't want your whole self." The caution stems from concerns that could arise about employees taking too many liberties in pulling their personal lives into their work environment. Also, given the vast range in employee ages, generational perspectives can be an issue. Older leaders may suspect that productivity is decreased during social networking activities, whereas Gen Y employees are comfortable navigating social media frequently and see the technology as a way to be more productive. Woodbury is treading carefully in establishing policies for the company's internal social networking platform. "As soon as the organization puts boundaries around the effort, it can be viewed as sinister and a means to control free expression. We certainly don't want to foster that perception."

Humana believes that enabling employees and leaders to see each other more clearly through the company's social networking site will improve Humana's ability to find quality successors. In addition, as employees are able to see each other's strengths and experience, they will be able to leverage the knowledge that resides throughout their networks. Humana values innovation, and this ability to tap specific expertise will encourage the exchange of new ideas among its workforce. Humana's purposeful efforts are certainly helping employees adapt to its changing landscape and to the world its customers live in.

TRAILBLAZER

Organizations everywhere are facing the same challenges as Humana. They are finding that the landscape around them is changing—both outside and inside their organizations— creating an urgent need for them to adapt for continued success.

In Chapter One, we briefly discussed that changes in three areas have been gaining momentum and have become more pressing in the past decade:

- *The nature of the business environment.* Leaders must operate in a much more complex environment. The world is becoming smaller as advancements in e-commerce, transportation, and communication have dissolved geographic borders that once distinguished businesses as "local" or "national"; any business can now be global.

- *Workforce demographics.* The composition of the workforce is changing in age, skill sets, and expectations. Legacy wisdom will be lost with the exodus of retirees.

- *Software technology that enables social connection.* The tools that have now cropped up both inside intranets and in local coffee shops have created new opportunities to facilitate communication and sharing.

These drivers are forcing organizations to look with a fresh perspective at the way they accomplish their goals. Like Humana, the best companies are actively implementing new ways to improve internal operations so that they can achieve success not only today but tomorrow. Many of the more proactive organizations are finding that the use of social media gives them more ways to work together, accelerates their productivity, and plays a part in developing a culture that will carry them into the future.

In this chapter, we'll examine these three drivers of change in greater depth and consider how social media can play a part in preparing organizations for success in this new landscape.

The Nature of the Business Environment

We have entered a new millennium, and we are facing a global business environment that is continually adjusting to accelerated change. In this unfamiliar territory, some economic opportunities may seem appealing, but the challenges can be equally daunting. The ways people relate to each other and the ways business is conducted are vastly different from those of just a few decades ago. Our environment is much more complex than ever before, globalization has made the planet a far more intimate workplace, and a fulfilling career no longer resembles traditional twentieth-century models. Let's take a closer look.

Growing Complexity

One characteristic of our new economy is that it has become much more complex in the past century. In his book *Powerful Times,*

Eamonn Kelly writes that this new reality is "messy, complex, and interconnected—and it is also increasingly volatile. It has been obvious for more than a decade that we live in an age of change; today, it appears that we are also living through a *change of age.*"[1] Kelly, CEO of Global Business Network, highlights seven *dynamic tensions*—paradoxical forces at play that increase the complexity of our world. For example, the huge shifts in business models and global trade paradigms that we are experiencing in the twenty-first century will have tremendous impact on more than just international commerce in coming years. The way we view power, commerce, and the acquisition or expenditure of resources has undergone monumental shifts in past centuries, and Kelly believes that we are currently in the midst of a knowledge-intensive economy with "far-reaching consequences for society, organizations and individuals."

Consider one example from the past century. On October 1, 1908, a new product rolled into the American way of life. The Model T was a bold example of innovation. With a steering wheel on the left side, a fully enclosed engine and transmission, and four cylinders cast in a single block, Henry Ford's new product was radical. But, as we know, it wasn't just the product that was novel, but also the way in which the product was made. Ford was revolutionary in his application of the assembly line for mass production of affordable cars for the common family. By 1913, the price of a touring Model T was $360, and sales had soared to 472,000. By 1918, half of all American cars were Model Ts. In 1931, Henry Ford surely had to grapple with human resource issues, supply chain challenges, and productivity dips, but if we consider his mantra "Any customer can have a car painted any color he wants so long as it's black," we can see how much simpler business was at the turn of the century.[2] Mass production was in style. Central to the success of this model of business operations were the known, predictable, repeatable, and standardized practices related to the deployment of human, mechanical, and material resources.

Today, organizational leaders must employ a very different set of operating assumptions. The primary approach to the creation of knowledge, goods, and services has advanced from mechanistic models to other perspectives. As a result of our changing times, our collective social frameworks for making sense of our world have also changed. For example, chaos theory, complexity theory, and systems thinking have become useful ways to view and describe the dynamic and seemingly chaotic and unpredictable world around us. Whether the subject is a business, a community, or a complex scientific problem, dynamics in the system are often mysterious, and cause and effect are not readily obvious. We've become increasingly concerned with creating *synergy*, the idea that the whole is somehow more than the sum of the parts. Indeed, it's often the relationship *between* the parts, their *interdependence*, that makes a difference.

With our minds tuned in to the natural complexity in our world, we realize that we actually control much less than we think we do. In any environment—business, personal, social—a dance is taking place among many interrelated forces. If we could sit on a high enough perch, we might see patterns that are currently invisible to us as we engage in the fray of daily systemic connections and interactions.

Imagine speeding along in a taxi on a congested dirt road in the busy city of Bangalore, India. You come to an intersection and shut your eyes, bracing yourself as your driver plunges into the melee. Emerging on the other side of the intersection, you breathe a sigh of relief. In a sense, those seemingly chaotic and unorganized moments could be analogous to the experience of navigating the "natural flow" of energy in the universe (and bumpers and honking horns) as it moves to music we can't hear with our ears. Organizations operate the same way. Healthy organizations are living systems that thrive through the establishment and maintenance of robust connections.

What does this mean for leaders in these changing times? Leaders must find ways to connect their employees across the many diverse parts of their organizations. At Oracle, senior executives have become aware of these dynamics in their global organizations. In a recent study, Kirsten Hanson of Oracle's Global Organization and Talent Development group looked at how these senior executives deal with the challenges of organizational complexity. Leaders in the study shared that the greatest challenges they face involve bringing employees together across multiple business disciplines and diverse perspectives. Specifically, they cited three challenges: (1) being able to effectively connect with virtual team members across time zones, (2) building collaboration and teamwork, and (3) operating effectively across geographies and functions.[3] These savvy and experienced leaders know that open and frequent communication is more critical than ever to cultivate connections between employees. Consequently, leveraging social networking tools could become a strategic differentiator in the effectiveness of their global operations, enabling them to foster a shared view of the organization's direction, greater collaboration, and faster innovation across the globe.

With the barrage of available information amplified by our new global reach, people are searching for ways to take advantage of their new capability without crashing from information overload. They have become "knowledge workers" in the information age. In an article for *CIO* magazine, Tom Davenport comments on the increased complexity with which the average knowledge worker must contend. He argues that to reduce the amount of technology they must interact with, workers are striving to *integrate* where possible: "In the past week, for example, I've met several people who have shifted to PDA/cell phone combo devices—not because they are cool gadgets, but because they hold the potential for simplifying life."[4]

It's a Small World After All

In 1995, a ten-year-old boy in California moved a joystick and watched a large video monitor. However, he wasn't playing a video game. He was reaching for artifacts on the *Titanic* ocean liner as it lay two-and-a-half miles below the surface of the North Atlantic. The robot he controlled was named Jason, and the boy was one of many "Argonauts" in the Jason Project, created by Dr. Robert Ballard, discoverer of the remains of the *Titanic*. For fourteen years Dr. Ballard, the Woods Hole Institute, and Electronic Data Systems, a global technology services company, have partnered to excite students across the globe about science and technology. More than a million youth and twenty-two thousand teachers have participated in the rigorous curriculum, culminating in a live expedition that uses their skills and knowledge. Students are selected to be part of the field team with Dr. Ballard, and thousands more participate virtually through *telepresence*—that is, by having live, online conversations with the field team from remote locations.

Those children will be well equipped for success in modern organizations. Business is now conducted around the clock and around the globe. Not so long ago, employees formed a community not only because of their work but also because they sat in the same building, walked to the same parking lot, and had lunch in the same cafeteria. Now it no longer matters where you sit. It matters that you have a cell phone, a keyboard, and an Internet connection. Tools that enable people to communicate and collaborate have made it possible for an employee to truly be a full participant in a global team. But with such a distributed workforce, companies still recognize the need for employees to feel that they belong to a larger whole. They know they must find ways to connect employees scattered across countries and working from remote offices, so that they have a sense of common identity, purpose, and shared cultural experience.

For global companies doing business every minute of every day, the requirement for real-time information becomes imperative. Such information enables better business decisions that lead to improved performance. Companies must be able to mine the knowledge of their employees for just-in-time delivery of the information needed, and they're looking to social media to help them in this effort.

The ability to be a global organization is not reserved only for large companies. As mentioned, anyone, anywhere, at any time can be global as long as she has an active Internet connection, which enables her to compete on the same playing field with any organization. Thomas Friedman refers to this new capability as Globalization 3.0. Globalization 1.0 was about *countries* becoming less protectionist, 2.0 was about *companies* becoming global as opposed to multinational, and 3.0 is about *individuals* extending themselves globally, or what he calls the "flat-world platform"[5]

The Blurring Career Life Cycle

When she was thirty-four years old, Joann Diaz left her job as a high school counselor to travel to South America for a year. When he was fifty-eight years old, Bill Slingland started his own consultancy for business continuity after a long career in engineering and program management. And when she was forty-five, Michele Iverson began her own business in landscape and design while still raising her three sons. Twenty years ago, these stories would have seemed unusual. The life cycle of a career used to be sequential, linear, and neatly segmented into three phases that you moved through dutifully. You were either not yet in the workforce, working, or retired. And there was a career ladder with rungs meant for climbing—going up, not down. Not necessarily so anymore.

For a variety of reasons, people are moving in and out of the workforce and redefining the career life cycle. Part-time work, job sharing, leaves of absence, outsourcing, contract work, and getting rehired have become common options that can benefit both employer and employee. In fact, a recent Nielsen study showed that the sixty-five years and older age group is the fastest-growing group in the career development category.[6] Trish Bharwada, recent retiree of the Dow Chemical Company, explains that retirees have deep knowledge of the organization and still have "a role to play with Dow."[7] People no longer feel that they must follow the old linear path; they can weave their way through a career that best suits their lifestyle and their changing needs and desires. Companies are therefore rethinking their traditional workforce planning assumptions and looking for ways to build a more flexible and longer-term relationship with employees. Robert Graber, CEO of WallStJobs.com, highlights the opportunity for businesses looking for experienced and successful candidates to fill positions. "Smart companies will look at these statistics and see opportunity," Graber said. "Interns can be any age. In fact, bringing in more seasoned interns can give your business the benefit of the candidate's vast experience while the intern develops new skills or business experience."[8] Job scaffolding has replaced the single ladder, allowing workers to move up, down, and sideways, affording them much more flexibility and creativity in their careers.

Susan Van Klink, executive vice president of SelectMinds, a social networking product and consulting company, argues that the employer-employee relationship is increasingly viewed as a *continuum* over a lifetime: "From the very first time someone enters your doors, . . . all the way through when they retire from the workforce altogether, there's a feeling of wanting to stay connected and wanting to tap into them throughout the lifecycle of their careers. . . to leverage them in many different ways." She asserts that social networking becomes a vehicle for maintaining connection in response to this paradigm shift.[9]

In the face of a changing business environment comprising increasing complexity, global and distributed workforces, and the blurring of a once distinct career life cycle, organizations are stepping back to understand the new world they inhabit and to understand where they will get the human resources needed for long-term viability. They'll continue to look further afield to the workforce around the globe.

The Shift in Workforce Demographics

Years ago, the pool of potential candidates from which organizations could draw was limited to the people in their local geographic area. But today that pool of candidates is of a truly global scope with an unprecedented composition.

Around the World

Let's take a quick look at the bigger picture of populations and where they reside across the planet. According to the International Data Base, our global population at the time of this writing is approximately 6.8 billion.[10] Where are these people? The top five most populous countries are

- China (about 1.3 billion)
- India (about 1.2 billion)
- United States (about 300 million)
- Indonesia (about 250 million)
- Brazil (about 200 million)

It's no wonder that the news media are continuously buzzing with stories about the changing business dynamics of China and India—their populations outnumber the next largest countries by vast margins, and modern technology is enabling them to interact more readily on the global stage. The world population doubled between 1959 and 1999. The U.S. population is expected to continue increasing, although at a slower growth rate, climbing to approximately nine billion in 2040.[11] Yet all this growth is deceiving. As one generation retires and another enters the workforce, we are actually entering into a global talent shortage. In this period of transition, organizations must be careful not to mistakenly operate with a "much more of the same" attitude. In fact, the characteristics of these transitioning generations are very diverse, a topic of discussion appearing on many executive agendas.

The Generation Factor

Generations are often defined by the major historical events that took place in members' lives, particularly during their younger years. These shared experiences shaped their mind-sets, beliefs, and behaviors.[12] We are entering an era during which we'll commonly have four generations actively in the workforce, and their differences present intriguing challenges for organizations trying to move forward at a pace that will beat the competition.

Much has been written about the generation factor, and each source delineates the generations using slightly different birth years. The following are not intended as stereotypes but to serve as general guidelines for our purposes, highlighting the span of birth years, the key events that shaped their belief system, and some of the more notable distinctions that are generally thought to characterize each distinctive generation.

- *Traditionalists, or the Silent Generation.* They make up roughly 7 percent of the global population. Born between 1900 and 1945, they experienced World War II and the Cuban Missile Crisis. They value stability and security.

- *Baby Boomers.* They constitute roughly 18 percent of the global population. Born between 1946 and 1964, they experienced the Viet Nam War and the assassinations of idealist leaders Martin Luther King Jr., John F. Kennedy, Robert F. Kennedy, and Malcolm X. They value teamwork and human rights.

- *Generation X.* They make up roughly 14 percent of the global population. Born between 1965 and 1976, and much fewer in number, they experienced a more peaceful time and saw more women enter the workforce while unemployment rose, and they experienced the dot-com bust. They value empowerment, are willing to rethink common rules, and demand corporate responsibility.

- *Generation Y, or the NetGen, Nexters, Echo Boomers, Millennials.* They compose roughly 24 percent of the global population. Born between 1977 and 2000, they have experienced a wide variety of random threatening events, from terrorist attacks to natural disasters, and the increasing alarm over the long-term health of the planet. They value technology, personal growth, and social activism.[13]

Organizations must understand the characteristics of each of the generations if they are to attract and retain the people essential to their success.

The War for Talent

As demographics shift, the impact on the workforce will be unavoidable. The Boomer generation, by far the largest until Gen Y came along, will soon be approaching the traditional retirement age. With the blurring of the career life cycle, we may see many of them continue working in some capacity, but the majority will probably leave their senior management roles in search of a work life with less stress. The Gen X population is smaller, and the effects of this have been felt as companies like Humana search for qualified successors for their key executive roles, currently filled by Traditionalists preparing to retire.

Demand is exceeding the supply of critical workers. A recent study shows an expected shortfall of ten million workers by the year 2010. Also, companies fear they will lose 50 percent of their seasoned management teams over the next five years, and unlike Humana, many will have no succession plans in place. They are therefore focusing on their talent management strategies to grow their existing employee capability. Because these organizations will be competing for precious new hires, they are also rethinking their talent acquisition strategies and focusing on how to entice the best Gen Y candidates.[14]

Many have sounded the alarm of an impending job crisis that will escalate through 2010 and beyond. By 2025, seventy-nine million workers, mostly of the Boomer generation, will have left the workforce in the United States alone. Only forty million will be entering. Some predictions include a shortage of five hundred thousand IT workers in India by 2010, highlighting the cross-cultural nature of this crisis. The impact will be powerful, prompting a growing concern that widespread labor shortages on the horizon have the power to cripple our socioeconomic infrastructure as we know it today.[15] But the Millennials are out there in large numbers. They will carry the baton that the previous generations hand off to them. As they move into the workforce, organizations must be ready to assimilate them effectively, and that begins with understanding the expectations of this generation.

The Millennial Connection

The significance of the Millennial generation in our organizations today and tomorrow cannot be overstated. This new generation of workers is changing the fundamental nature of how and where work is performed. First, there are the sheer numbers of them—roughly two billion globally. In the United States alone, those born between the years 1980 and 2000 number more than seventy-five million. Second, this generation could be characterized as an extremely diverse workforce: almost 40 percent in the United States are of non-Caucasian descent. Third, new emerging social norms may be somewhat different than those held by the Traditionalists and Boomers—for example, that of the "nuclear family." Nearly 25 percent of Millennials were raised in single-family homes, and 75 percent had working mothers with smaller families.[16]

But most notable is this generation's comfort with technology. Millennials have grown up with laptop computers, cell phones, and video games. They've never known a world without electronic payments, texting, or instant messaging. In fact, they want everything instantly, as they instinctively recognize the fleeting shelf life of information. Millennials will demand convenience in information access and real-time communication that satisfies their need for instant knowledge. They have been called "digital natives" because they are connected through their laptops and cell phones, and use these tools as second nature.[17] Steve Snyder, IT program manager at Intel Corporation, emphasizes the point that younger employees are expecting instant and integrated ways to communicate throughout their personal and work environments: "This is not just about being social. We hear this request across the board in all business functions. An employee wants to know how she can take her smart mobile device today and connect it to her e-mail. It is simply expected. She believes it should be mandatory. We need to enable this connection and provide it in a secure environment."

It has been estimated that those between eighteen and twenty-four years old spend about ten hours online per week. And these users are all about connecting. About 22 percent of this generation check social networking sites daily, and they make up the bulk of social networking users on six of the most popular social networking sites.[18] Indeed, they will eventually utilize social networking even more than television and cellular phones. One study by Fox Interactive has found that as social networking site use increases among Millennials, television, cell phone, and video game use decreases almost proportionately.[19]

Millennials Make a Difference

Millennials have also been hailed as the generation that will make the greatest contribution. Witnessing their parents, the Boomer generation, enslaved to work, Generation Y will insist on flexibility, work-life balance, and corporate social responsibility. Some say that whereas Generation X *argues* for corporations to take more social responsibility, the Millennials will *do* something about it.

Clearly, this generation will be unlike others in motivation, purpose, outlook, and expectations. They will value continuous learning, trust, and flexibility. Millennials are most likely to view the world as an interconnected and interdependent ecosystem. However, they will trust people, not institutions. Friends will have a strong influence on Generation Y, perhaps more so than for other generations.[20] They will demand flatter organizational structures and communication, and will be less loyal to companies as a whole. Moreover, many Millennials have been raised as a product of the "positive psychology" movement and, in many cases, some will come into the workforce with a sense that effort is equal to achievement.

It is important to recognize the distinct attitude that Gen Y has toward work. The adage "They work to live, rather than live to work" is probably true for this group. In fact, unlike the generations before them, they are not afraid to leave an organization if they are not getting what they need. In one survey, 77 percent of Gen Y workers say that social aspects of work are very important to their satisfaction on the job, and 21 percent report leaving a job because they felt disconnected.[21] The challenge for companies will be to create cultural contexts that can cater to the demands of this generation while continuing to ensure high performance and continuity of execution. But they must meet this challenge; there is no alternative. A few years from now in workplaces everywhere, Boomers will exit in increasingly large numbers. At some point, Gen Xers will move into the top management jobs, although there won't be enough of them to fill Boomer shoes. Millennials will have a growing presence in the workforce, and they will have a need to be connected, which must be met by the organizations that will depend on their contributions.

Software for Social Connection

Two employees bump into each other in the hallway. "Hey Bob, did you read Maria's blog on improving the restocking process?" "No, I didn't, but thankfully Jenny did and tweeted the top two changes that need to be made. I put the word out to the inventory group on LinkedIn, and Joe IM'd me to say that he had already commented on her blog and started a forum to keep the discussion alive. Forty-two people have already gone to the wiki and added some great changes to her process document that should speed up the—oh! Lee is texting that the web conference is about to start."

A short decade ago, if you had passed these two in the hallway, you would have thought they were speaking in another language. The way we communicate has been transformed as new technologies and social media make it easy to stay connected every moment of the day and night. The use of these tools has become commonplace in every Internet-ready country. Let's look at where these tools are used, how people choose to engage with them, and how organizations are beginning to capitalize on the phenomenon of social media.

The Proliferation of Social Media

If you have secretly been thinking that the social media frenzy is simply a passing fad or a set of activities reserved for a niche group of technocrats, consider these statistics about the percentage of people using social media tools across the globe:[22]

- Read blogs: Japan, 52%; South Korea, 31%; United States, 25%
- Comment on blogs: South Korea, 21%; Japan, 20%; United States, 14%
- Use Wikipedia at least monthly: United States, 22%
- Watch user-created video: United States, 29%; Japan, 20%; United Kingdom, 17%
- Visit social networking sites: South Korea, 35%; United States, 25%; United Kingdom, 21%

It's undeniable that the use of social media has become a global phenomenon. At the heart of all social media use is the need to connect with others to exchange information, and social networking sites are specifically aimed at connecting people who were previously unaware of each other. When we look at geographic regions, the highest use of social networking is in Asia, which makes up 35 percent of the total online population. As a whole, Europe, the Middle East, and Africa (EMEA) are a close second with 38 percent of users; North America is at 25 percent; and Latin America makes up 12 percent.[23] Interestingly, over a thirty-day period, 55 percent of regular Internet users in Korea accessed a social networking site, as compared to only 24 percent of the comparable U.S. population.[24] As reported in a study by Datamonitor, "In South Korea, a single service (Cyworld) already has 18 million accounts—enough for 30 percent of the entire country's population. Social networking sites are 'sticky,' too, as users keep coming back to check up on friends and acquaintances."[25]

And, as you might imagine, the younger users are pulling these numbers up with increasing speed. A recent report including sixty-one hundred library users in the United States, Canada, France, Germany, Japan, and the United Kingdom noted that among college students, 48 percent report using a social media site in general, 56 percent report viewing a social networking site, and 59 percent read blogs.[26] In another study, 41 percent of people between ages eighteen and thirty-four described themselves as casual users of social networking sites, and 24 percent described themselves as active users.[27] According to the Conference Board, about half of all social networking users visit sites on a daily basis: "Half of these people say they log on several times a day. Among other household members, those age 12 to 17 are more likely than their siblings to be daily users, with 57 percent saying they frequent social networking sites at least once a day."[28]

In the early years of social networking, people were skeptical that it would stick. In 2005, CNET writer Molly Wood predicted the demise of this mode of communicating, saying that the "word on the street is that social networking is in trouble."[29] Yet social networking use has continued to grow every year thereafter. ComScore, Inc., a company that specializes in measuring the digital world, reported that social networking site use increased 25 percent globally between June 2007 and June 2008.[30]

Who Gives, Who Takes, and Who Watches

To understand more about the ways social media can be used in organizations, let's look at how different types of employees are taking advantage of these tools.

The use of social media can take many forms, and people interact with these tools in a variety of ways. As in all social interactions, some people initiate, others respond, and others stand on the sidelines and observe. Of course, being a spectator is easy, so it's not surprising that most people will be found in this group: 48 percent of Americans, 37 percent of Europeans, and 66 percent of Japanese and Chinese fall into this category. We all know that there is also a segment of people who love to join organizations but may never attend a meeting, lead a project, or collect signatures on a petition. They also appear in the world of social media: 25 percent of the global online population has joined social networking sites. For those who love to respond to the thoughts of others, blogs, online forums, and wikis are places for them to share their views as a collaborator, critic, or advocate. One in five Americans, one in four Europeans, and one in three Japanese fall into this category.

You can imagine that younger people, both men and women, are more active in all areas than the older generations and continually skew the averages. For example, women in Generation Y are much more likely to use social media than the average American, but they still don't use these tools quite as much as Gen Y men. It seems that men are slightly more likely than women to initiate interaction, comment on others' material, or stand by and observe. However, when it comes to joining social networking sites, the two genders show up in equal numbers.[31]

Organizations can use this demographic information to better understand the probable preferences of their own workforce. Depending on a company's employee population, it might be risky to equate a low volume of content postings to the failure of a social networking initiative. In fact, employees of all generations are participating in their own way. Among the Traditionalists, those who initiate may be few, but spectators may be many. Boomer managers will need these tools to help promote a shared view of strategy while maintaining independent thought. Generation Xers are quite tech savvy; they do gravitate to social networking as well as other ways to express their opinions and respond to ideas in the social media space. And, make no mistake, Millennials will demand the provision of social media tools to do their jobs. Incorporating these tools into an organization's normal workflow can serve as a catalyst for intergenerational communication, creating new vehicles to develop shared perspectives and speed the achievement of common goals.

Your Competitors Get It—Do You?

What does all this mean for leaders who desire to build organizations that excel today as well as tomorrow? The answer is simple: social media connects people. It enables communication, collaboration, and the sharing of vital information that employees need to do their jobs better and faster. It can reinforce a global mind-set among management teams, ensuring an equality of perspectives and the inclusion of a diversity of voices.

But social media tools are new for most of us over the age of thirty. Successful leaders who have built strong organizations by taking prudent risks may still be hesitant. But the time for "wait and see" has already passed. Chances are, your competitors are already using social media as a vehicle to enhance speed of execution and to take advantage of the previously untapped energy and ideas of their employees.

A recent report describes how employers are sanctioning the use of social media in their organizations during working hours. Whereas 37 percent allowed the use of social media in 2007, the 2008 data showed 69 percent of businesses opening the doors to social media.[32] The report details that 75 percent of employees are already using such social networking sites as MySpace, Facebook, and LinkedIn for business purposes, up 15 percent from 2007. And they are bringing the advantages inside the organization by creating internal communities. Leaders, HR professionals, and organization development consultants are taking action, in the best way they know how: 63 percent of organizations are using outward-facing social media to build their brand with customers; 61 percent are using internal social media strategies to improve communication and collaboration. Many organizations are creating specific roles to ensure the effective integration of social media, in a way that truly helps employees take full advantage of these tools. Laurie Buczek is the social computing program manager at Intel. She says, "Intel sees the use of social computing as a critical enabler for our employees. I am solely focused on how to do this right on the inside, how to bring these tools in to the company for our employees to use as a way to transform the way we are collaborating, connecting, and communicating today."

Another company that has taken advantage of social media and focusing its efforts is Dow. Trish Bharwada previously managed My Dow Network, a social networking site that expands Dow's employee community. Here's how Dow's story unfolds.

Trailblazer—Dow Connects with Employees, Past and Present

TRAILBLAZER

Charlie studied the Web page carefully before clicking on the Job Opportunities link. It had been six months since he retired, but he found that he didn't go golfing as much as he thought he would. In fact, he didn't do many of the things he longed to do during his working years. Even though it was really nice to know that he could golf or build wine racks or spend time in the garden, the truth was that he missed being at work. After twenty-six years with Dow, he felt he was truly valued by the company and his colleagues. Although he had been in management, he was still sought out by many for his hands-on expertise in operations. In fact, he had informally mentored two newer employees who he felt were destined to play a critical role in Dow's future success. Charlie missed feeling that he was making a difference, and he had to admit that he missed being connected to an organization that was making a difference in the grand scheme of things.

So he felt hopeful as he went to the My Dow Network Web site. He was hopeful that he would find an opportunity to stay involved with Dow in some way. He had heard from a few of his old friends who had also retired. At first, they came here to find the information they needed to make the transition from employee to retiree. But now they came to the site to see what was happening at Dow and to read about other retirees and Dow alumni. They found that this kept them connected to the community that was still so much a part of them. They were the ones who told Charlie about the Job Opportunities link.

Although the individuals in this scenario are fictitious, the story is real, the situation common. Dow recognized the power of social networking and wanted to tap that power in building a rich human resource community that could continue to participate in the company's success. In 2007, Dow was feeling the pain of inescapable truths. Its executives knew that over the next five years, 40 percent of their workforce would likely retire, taking their Dow knowledge and experience with them. They also knew that they would not be able to meet the hiring demands that such a drain would leave them with. Other companies would experience the same challenge and would be vying for the same young talent to join their workforce, and the ramp-up time would surely cause a dip in their productivity. The Dow leaders believed that greater employee engagement would increase retention of key talent, and they were convinced that enabling employees to connect with each other was an essential strategy in improving employee engagement. And finally, they found it increasingly difficult to find, hire, and retain top-notch female employees. They already had great women's programs in place for more than twenty years, but they felt it was time to rejuvenate them to better compete for these precious resources.[33]

In December 2007, Dow launched My Dow Network to cultivate four Dow communities: retirees, alumni, current employees, and women. The official news release described the site as follows: "The closed, online community allows users to expand their professional networks, renew old friendships, stay connected with the latest Dow information, and explore new job opportunities. It also keeps Dow connected to a larger talent pool, fuels collaboration and innovation, and facilitates a diverse and inclusive work environment."[34] Before its release in an August 2007 *Computerworld* article, Kevin Small, leader of Dow's Global Resource Management Center, was quoted as saying, "The intent is to increase engagement with the overall Dow family—current and former employees—and allow them to stay connected and stay current on what Dow is doing in case they choose to return." For women, Small describes the network as an informal way for them to keep in touch with mentors and peers to get information about reentering the work force, articles, or balancing child-rearing and work life.[35]

The retiree network alone offers many benefits to users. It was designed to include a search engine to identify other retirees, alumni, and employees with a spotlight section to share who returned to Dow and how they lend their experience and contributine in new ways. The network was also designed to feature timely news to the community with targeted information and resources most valuable to them (discounts, invitations to company events, and a forum for posing questions to the community and likewise to responding to each other's inquiries).

Within the first three months, eight hundred retirees found their way to the site, creating more than three hundred thousand connections and initiating twelve thousand targeted searches.[36] Since then, the community has continued to grow. Retirees, like our imaginary Charlie, have found their opportunity to remain engaged. They've found the information they need, broadened their own network of people and resources, and become better ambassadors for Dow in the world beyond the company doors. Dow benefits as well by keeping its valuable knowledge workers closer to "home," involving them in an ongoing way, and creating a bridge between the new employees and the legacy knowledge.

My Dow Network is one of many efforts Dow created to build an engaged workforce that spans the more complex career life cycle we mentioned earlier. As a play on its roots in chemistry, Dow proudly shows Hu^8, a new symbol on its own imaginary periodic table that depicts "the Human Element." Its Web site describes it this way in a captivating video: "the missing element is the human element, and when we add it to the equation the chemistry changes. Every reaction is different. . . . The human element is the element of change. It gives us our footing to stand fearlessly and face the future."[37] Dow is truly trying to unleash the human element in its workforce by finding new ways to enable people to contribute and add value. Dow's online outreach is proving to be key to its employee engagement efforts.

TRAILBLAZER

Get on Board

In this book we share many examples of such organizations as Dow and Intel that understand how social media can help them achieve their most complex business, workforce, and technology issues.

We have been energized by these forward-thinking organizations that are jumping into the twenty-first century with excitement and a sense of purpose, leveraging social media to foster a win-win for employees, customers, and the sustained success of their business. Their passion is contagious. They are out of the gate and running. But before they travel too far down any one path, one of the first steps in their journey is to become familiar with the many new social media technologies available. The next chapter will equip you with the basics of the most common social media technologies. From there, we'll share in Chapter Four how specific organizations are putting these tools into action.

Join the Conversation

Connect with others who, like you, are exploring, experimenting, and pioneering the use of social media to propel organizational performance. Go to www.socialmediaatwork-connection.com to ask your questions, learn what others are doing, and add your insights to the conversation. This chapter raises the following questions for you and your fellow community members:

- What are the drivers that are compelling you to use social media in your organization?
- How have you made a business case for the value of social media in your organization?
- What do you know about the social media needs and habits of your workforce?

3

WHAT IS SOCIAL MEDIA, AND HOW DOES IT WORK?

The Association of Test Publishers (ATP) is a nonprofit trade association representing developers and providers of tests, assessment tools, and services related to education, employment, certification, licensing, and clinical uses.[1] Established in 1992, ATP serves as an advocate for the testing community by establishing professional guidelines, disseminating information, and educating the public about the benefits of properly administered tests.

The ATP Board wanted the association to have a central repository so that members could dynamically find and update information about specific topics of interest. Because ATP's members are geographically dispersed, they needed a centralized method of hosting industry-specific knowledge. The establishment of a wiki resulted in such a community tool to share valuable information among its members. One topic that members often seek resources for is test security. Key reference data—such as bibliographies on test security, useful links, meeting minutes and notes, hints on intellectual property theft, and test administration tips—were added to this central repository.

The ATP has now established a rich set of social media solutions that address these needs. Each of the ATP's five divisions includes publishers of professional certification and licensure exams and other entities with an interest in test security. In addition to the association's central repository of knowledge on the wiki, each division also has its own set of working documents on the wiki where members post notes, receive feedback, and share ideas on how to make test security better. Along the way, the ATP has learned how to make its wiki environment more valuable to members. For example, the association discovered that members preferred their wiki environment to be "padlocked" so that only members could access the information. The organization also found that it needed to continue educating its members on how to use the wiki and how to derive the most benefit from it.

The impact? Active ATP Jamie Mulkey, Ed.D., underscores that the test security wiki shows members, "We're into technology, we're using it; we're forward-thinkers; it's a great example of a tangible member benefit!" Through social media, the ATP can confidently showcase the work its members do and the value that the association brings to them.

ATP's use of social computing technologies has enabled it to speed up its communication and elicit broad perspectives from members much faster than it could with traditional e-mail and meeting methods. Aside from the speed of obtaining relevant information, there has been an increase in the consistency and quality of members' work, as social media has provided a new method by which to connect and collaborate with test experts. Members also feel as if they belong to a larger community, which gives them a sense of greater personal and professional benefit.

Throughout 2008, the global television network CNBC ran a popular commercial for Wachovia Bank (now a part of Wells Fargo) featuring a series of examples of the need for human connection: "She's with me." "I'm with the band." "I'm with them."

Everyone wants to "be with" others. The need for connection and community is deeply ingrained in our human psyche. Connection gives us a sense of identity, a purpose, and a feeling of belonging. Perhaps each of us has a deep and unconscious awareness that we are all connected at some level; meeting each other face-to-face need not be a criterion.

We have seen how people's need to feel connected can drive the formation of a never-ending list of affinity groups that share information around common interests. In a sense, the ATP is one such group finding benefit in being part of a community. At the core of affinity groups is the desire to share ideas, ask questions, and to give and receive help in achieving goals. Just as people have learned to turn to public search engines for answers to questions on just about any topic, they are also learning that other individuals are just as viable a source of information. In many cases, getting the information from other people is better because it comes with intangible added value: context, experience, and opinion. When one is in new territory or creating something new, the ability to find people who can help is priceless. Again, the bottom line of social media is that it *enables people to connect, communicate, and collaborate*. In organizations, the potential for greater productivity and improved long-term performance is huge, but the question of how to begin can often be overwhelming. In Chapters Four and Five we'll see many examples of how organizations are using social media, but let's first lay the foundation with a shared understanding of major types of social media. This chapter focuses on demystifying social media as well as creating more familiarity with the most common technologies and how they work.

What Is Social Media?

Lana, fifty-three, a seasoned and very well educated corporate recruiter for a large aerospace company, sat across the table and asked in a hushed voice, "OK, what exactly is 'Web 2.0'? Is it an application? A platform? A coding language?" She's not alone in her confusion. A new vocabulary, rife with ambiguity, is in play. Many terms, such as Web 2.0, social technology, social computing, and social media, are often used interchangeably. In this book, we have focused on the term *social media,* defining it as the various electronic tools available to help accelerate and improve our ability to connect, communicate, and collaborate.

Much of what we commonly regard today as social media began in 1997 with a social networking site called www.SixDegrees.com that brought people together online.[2] The site shut down in 2000; it was just a bit ahead of its time, and people were not yet accustomed to sharing information so publicly. Despite its demise, Six Degrees established many of the common characteristics that we see in social networking sites and other forms of social media. Today, social media encompasses all the Internet-enabled capabilities for communicating through different means—audio, video, text, images, and every other combination or permutation imaginable. As new users become familiar with these tools, they are frequently overwhelmed by the process of determining which tool is "right" for them. Some may even question whether some tools are here to stay or are passing fads.

Regardless of longevity, these tools are becoming increasingly popular and are accessible to anyone with an Internet connection. They are becoming ever more embedded in our everyday lives.

The Key Players in Social Media

To understand the key "players" of social media, let's look at a few more closely so that you will recognize some of the "paints" available for your "palette." We refer to blogs, wikis, and social networking sites as "the big three" because they seem to be the most prevalent forms of social media in use today. Considering the growth and development rate of these tools, we know that the big three will soon change, and other forms of social media will rise to the top. But for now, these technologies are representative of the huge variety of tools available for connecting people online. Beyond the big three, we will touch on a few other tools among the potpourri of most commonly used social media as well.

In each of the next sections, we begin with a plain and simple definition of the tool and follow this with a description of the way it works, common uses, and just a glimpse of its uses within organizations. We'll share many more examples of organizational uses in Chapters Four and Five. We've included usage percentages in these descriptions, and unless otherwise noted, these statistics came from Forrester's North American Social Technographics Online Survey, which included more than ten thousand U.S. consumers.[3]

Blog

Plain and simple: an individual's journal that he makes public for all to see, inviting responsive comments from his readers.

The word *blog* is actually short for "web log." The author writes about topics he is passionate about, topics he wants others to learn about, or perhaps simply his curious musings for the day. The frequency of blog entries, called posts, depends on the topic and the blogger. Several tools exist that can enable anyone to create his or her own blog, Blogger.com being perhaps the most commonly known. According to Forrester's survey, 11 percent of U.S. adult consumers publish, maintain, or update a blog.

Readers of a blog can weigh in with comments, augmenting the blogger's ideas, praising them, or critiquing them. The ability of readers to respond to other people's comments creates a true asynchronous conversation. Of course, not everyone comments. In fact, whereas 25 percent of U.S. adults read blogs, only 14 percent comment on someone else's blog.

The primary purpose of a blog is for the author (blogger) to share his or her views. Large organizations also use blogs to communicate to their customers, establishing a point of view and shaping the brand they desire. But that's an external use of corporate blogs. There are a variety of uses for blogs *inside* organizations.

Inside the organization. Developing a shared sense of corporate direction is difficult. For the executive of a large company, blogs can be an opportunity to reach employees with a more personal touch. A blog carries a much more collegial tone than an e-mail blast addressed to the masses. Inside organizations, blogs are useful for sharing the views of executive leaders, project leaders, key influencers, experts, or group representatives. A blog can also be an effective learning tool: training participants can blog their analyses of a strategic problem. For example, IBM executives have public journals (similar to blogs) to share their goals, the actions they've taken, and the lessons they've learned along the way.

In nonprofit and volunteer organizations, blogs provide a great way for leaders to inspire and engage the team. This virtual way of "rallying the troops" can also provide just-in-time information and continuous feedback regarding the value of team members' efforts. Guest bloggers from within the blog's community can offer their posts to show appreciation and inform the team of the impact they have made. Responding comments further solidify the commitment of the team when they describe the rewarding feelings they have experienced from knowing their efforts made a difference.

Wiki

Plain and simple: a Web site where multiple people can collaborate to create a work together by easily adding to or editing the content of the site.

Ward Cunningham remembers an employee at the Honolulu International Airport telling him to take the "wiki wiki shuttle" bus to speed between airport terminals, explaining that *wiki* is Hawaiian for "quick." The name stuck with him, and he chose it over the less interesting label of "quick web" to name his creation. He debuted it on the Internet on March 25, 1995.[4]

Wikis offer a common Web space for a group of people to create a project together. Wikipedia, perhaps the most widely recognized wiki, is an open invitation for anyone to educate others on any topic. If you look up the word *wiki* on Wikipedia, you will find the following definition: "a page or collection of Web pages designed to enable anyone who accesses it to contribute or modify content, using a simplified markup language. Wikis are often used to create collaborative websites and to power community websites."[5]

Although such descriptions emphasize the ability to create Web sites, collaborators on a wiki more commonly use it as a working space to create documents for planning, brainstorming, research, or building on ideas. It just so happens that this flexible document ends up as a Web page.

Many available free tools allow anyone to create a wiki, wikispaces.com and pbwiki.com being among the most common. Although some wiki tools call for knowledge of basic skills in html (hypertext markup language), many do not require any special skills at all. The creator, usually referred to as the administrator, simply names the wiki and begins to create pages. He can add pages, link to other pages within the wiki or outside it, and create a navigation menu, all with the click of his mouse. In addition, most wiki tools allow the administrator and any contributor to add files of any type (photos, documents, video, and so on) that can be seen or downloaded by visitors.

What's happening on the other side of the Internet connection? The administrator lets his community know that the wiki is available for their input, and they, too, can edit each page, adding to each other's contributions or changing them as they prefer. Although errors in information can sometimes occur, the content is validated and corrected by the users themselves.

Wikis have three basic privacy settings. Public wikis allow the public to view and edit the wiki. Protected wikis allow the public to view the wiki, but limit edits to named members of that wiki community. In private wikis, viewing and editing are available only to members. Some now include a fourth privacy setting that enables the administrators to customize view and edit rights for each member of the community.

Discussion pages are another feature of wikis. These serve as a sort of parallel practice space or scribble pad where contributors justify their edits or have a dialogue to discuss what should be included or not. E-mail notifications are automatically sent to the administrator to alert him that changes have been made to specific pages.

Wikis are being used in a variety of ways. As we saw with ATP, nonprofits can use them to share a wide variety of information and engage their workforce or volunteers in common goals, or provide them with common tools and resources. The scientific community has also found benefit in using wikis. For example, Wikipedia hosts a huge site dedicated to the human genome project, and its discussion page is a treasure trove of innovative thought. Steven L. Salzberg writes on the PubMed Central Web site that the annotation of genomes becomes outdated over time, presenting a substantial challenge to the genome research community. He suggests wikis as a useful solution: "A 'genome wiki' might provide just the solution we need for genome annotation. A wiki would allow the community of experts to work out the best name for each gene, to indicate uncertainty where appropriate and to discuss alternative annotations."[6]

Inside the organization. Within organizations, wikis enable collaboration on a grand scale. It used to be common for work teams to be located under the same roof. But globalization, lifestyle changes, and technology have combined to create a workforce that is scattered across geographies and rarely seated across the table from one another. Myriad tools exist to help the members of organizations—corporate and nonprofit, large and small—work together, despite the challenge of distance and differing time zones. A wiki is one such tool.

For example, the University of San Francisco used a wiki to research and determine which wiki tool the school should use. The task force of faculty was asked to research a variety of wiki tools and comment on a wiki with their analysis of the benefits and drawbacks of each option. The wiki enabled faculty to learn together, sharing discoveries and ideas about how to incorporate a whole host of Web 2.0 tools into their faculty communities and to improve their effectiveness as instructors.

Let's turn to civic organizations. In New Zealand, the minister of police recognized that their governing bible, the Police Act, was outdated and inadequate to serve as a guideline for the modern environment. The Police Act sets forth how policing happens in New Zealand, provides for the existence of the national police service, and delineates how it is to operate. The Police Act of 1958 had been revised more than twenty-five times in an ongoing effort to keep aligned with the changing needs of New Zealand. There comes a point when, as with many sources of truth, revisions can obscure the effectiveness and original intent of the document. Therefore, the government launched a comprehensive effort to revise the Police Act. The effort involved many rounds of input from specialized consultants, government representatives, the police force, and the general public. In September 2007, a wiki was added to the process as an innovative way to collect public opinion and ideas regarding the new Police Act. The source of input spanned the globe as international contributors gave suggestions on all aspects of New Zealand's policing structure—overarching operations as well as daily processes. The input gathered from the "wiki Act," as it came to be known, was added to the other sources of input, and was instrumental in creating the revised Police Act of October 1, 2008.[7]

In so-called enterprise wikis, corporations are often looking for the efficiency or cost savings to be found in implementing a wiki solution. Although wikispaces.com and pbwiki.com are common wiki tools, Twiki.org and Socialtext.com are two tools commonly used inside larger companies to create robust wikis that are secured within their firewalls. Twiki bills itself as a flexible, powerful, and easy-to-use enterprise wiki, enterprise collaboration platform, and knowledge management system. It is known as a structured wiki, typically used to run a project development space, a document management system, a knowledge base, or any other groupware tool, on an intranet or on the Internet, to create wikis for internal use only. Similarly, Socialtext is an organization that offers a variety of "social software" to help companies gain efficiencies and harness the collective genius of its employees. Its toolkit includes social networking, wiki workspaces, web logs dashboards, social messaging, and distributed spreadsheets.

Social Networking Site

Plain and simple: a Web site that allows people to share information about themselves and to search for others for the purpose of giving information, receiving information, or forming beneficial relationships.

Our working definition is intentionally simple; it includes the basic human character, the critical element of Internet technology, and the broad variety of purposes and objectives of those participating. We believe that social networking sites are a key form of social media that have the benefit of extending beyond "old-fashioned" networking techniques by targeting an audience, allowing exponential reach, and illuminating hidden "gifts."

Not Your Grandmother's Networking.   In the book *Networking Magic*, Frishman and Lublin describe networking as grounded in relationships: "It's the development of a team that will support your efforts and the efforts of your network teammates to reach your respective goals. Networking is about forging bonds and sharing. It's connecting with people who have common interests and objectives and generously give to one another."[8]

A little technology changes everything. In the "old days"— you know, a decade ago—when we wanted to give information, receive information, or form beneficial relationships, we would join the Kiwanis Club, the Rotary Club, the local country club, or the local Leads Group. This was the means by which we found people who might share a common interest or help us achieve our goals, large and small. More often, these people might know someone *else* who has the information we seek.

Although social networking has its roots in the good old-fashioned networking methods known to the generations before us, the boost from Internet technology transforms it into a speedy and targeted way to find the right person or the information you seek. These transformations are all around us—for example, newspaper classifieds became eBay and craigslist. A flyer stapled to a telephone pole became Upcoming.com, a searchable Web site for sharing events and meetings in the community. Finding the right bank loan became Zopa.com, a "social lending" site that connects individual lenders and borrowers. Job fairs became Hotjobs.com and Monster.com, job search sites.

What's happening in these transformations? Technology has enabled a process that was once a bit random, slow, and limited to become one that is targeted and lightning fast, with reach that extends to anyone on the planet with an Internet connection.

Targeted Audiences. Social networking sites enable a variety of people to form groups of common interest. When you have ideas or questions, you can pose them to communities who are already formed within a site, and receive hundreds of replies very quickly. Even though you may not know the group members personally, your request for information has been targeted to those who are most likely to have answers for you.

Unexpected Reach. Another characteristic that social networking techniques provide is the opportunity for unexpected reach. For example, if you posted your question on LinkedIn's affinity group for members of the Organization Development Network, it could be viewed by twenty-eight hundred or more people. However, any one of those individuals might forward that question on to his or her personal network. Because everyone's network is a different size, the possible connections vary, but the exponential growth is astonishing. For example, one person with a personal network of a hundred people can lead to 1.6 million connections if a question is forwarded by each member of the network community.

Identifying and Illuminating Hidden Gifts. Michelangelo believed that the final image of his sculpture was trapped within the block of marble, hidden until he could reveal it by removing the rock that surrounds it. Social networking strategies work the same way within organizations. Once a question is posed to a larger group or an informal leader emerges, those who can contribute come out of the woodwork to provide ideas or to comment on a blossoming solution. They're attracted to the topics for which they have "gifts to lend" or an interest to share. It's as though they break through the surrounding organization that keeps them hidden, emerging for the right purpose at the right time.

Today, people who engage in conversation via social networking sites are typically searching for "friends" and "acquaintances" or for a purposeful interaction with someone specific. An *online profile* is a social resume that gives others a snapshot of who you are. With profiles as the primary structure, social networking sites enable participants to connect with others who are part of a vast web of relationships.

Often this type of networking results in special interest groups, known as *affinity groups* or communities of practice. These relationships can link people on the basis of shared interests, activities, and goals. Most important, the power of social networking lies in its ability to tap a network that was previously unavailable without the aid of Internet technology. Many social networking sites allow users to view their own networks and also the networks of their friends, the networks of those friends, and so on.

A plethora of social networking sites support a vast range of interests and practices. The three most popular sites are MySpace, Facebook, and LinkedIn, which attract millions of users who access specific Internet links on a daily basis. Although anyone can use a social networking site for multiple purposes, each site naturally caters to a specific audience.

For example, MySpace is geared toward teens, and approximately 88 percent of its users are under age thirty-five.[9] Facebook initially attracted younger users. Currently, approximately 90 percent of its users are under thirty-five years old,[10] but it is gaining older users and enterprise users as well. LinkedIn is aimed at a professional audience who are seeking jobs, resources, or specific information to help with their work or career aspirations.

By participating on a social networking Web site, you are implicitly inviting others to reach out to you for any reason they find of interest. Reading the profiles of others therefore facilitates quick and painless introductions. This implicit norm makes it particularly easy for somewhat shy individuals to connect with others.

Many early adopters of social networking sites in the United States were born after 1964. In other words, Generation Xers, born between 1965 and 1976, were the first group to grow up exploring the new capabilities of the Internet. As discussed in Chapter Two, Millennials, who were born after 1977, grew up comfortable with the Internet and the gadgetry of modern communications technology. These young users spurred the success of MySpace and Facebook, the sites with by far the most overall usage in this age group. As of April 2009, MySpace held approximately 32 percent of the users among the top ten social network sites. The same data show Facebook with about 27 percent of users. Although this is a huge portion of young users, many anticipate that these numbers will decrease as these users become older and develop more sophisticated networking needs.[11]

The popularity and growth in use of social networking sites are astounding. Reporting total usage numbers probably makes little sense because the numbers grow exponentially each day. According to Marty Fahncke, author and Internet marketing specialist, Facebook alone gains 250,000 people each week. In addition, one in four online American adults use at least one social networking site.[12]

Inside the organization. Whereas most organizations are structured by function, geography, services, or products, social networking cuts across these artificial boundaries to "flatten" communications. Challenges, problems, and opportunities usually require frequent information sharing within organizations. In truth, this information does not typically follow a vertical path, flowing down the organizational chart's clean hierarchy and reporting structure. Instead, the most effective and speedy problem solving involves useful information that emerges from the in-between, with an unstructured and informal meandering. This nebulous place is often referred to as the "white space," and the communication that occurs here is often horizontal and flat. Social networking sites can help facilitate this kind of lateral communication, ignoring traditional structures that limit free flow of information, making it available to all.

Other common uses inside organizations center around project work, succession planning, talent management, and knowledge management. Imagine how any of these efforts would gain speed and depth if all employees had a profile that shared critical information: key skills, passionate interests, industry experience, global experience, languages spoken, leadership roles, performance review ratings, kudos from colleagues, project successes, key accomplishments, biggest lessons learned, work styles, external affiliations, and so on. In Chapter Two we saw how Humana is exploring the use of an internal social networking tool similar to Facebook. With an extensive profile for each employee, Humana would have a rich source of knowledge for talent management and succession planning efforts. We explore more of these opportunities further in Chapter Four and Five.

Discussion Forum

Plain and simple: a place where questions can be posed to the public or a specific community and then answers and threaded comments can be viewed by all.

Discussion forums resemble the "threaded chat" that was so popular in the 1990s, especially in universities and research teams. Forums allow individuals to have a quick, just-in-time, meaningful exchange about a question, suggestion, recommendation, or rating. Retailers understood the value of discussion forums early on. Buying furniture at Target? Read the reviews and the responses of customers to learn which items look like fine furniture and which are a disappointment.

Inside the organization. Discussion forums provide a great way to find answers to common questions. Just as they do in the outside world, people within organizations are seeking empathy and answers, and their colleagues are eager to provide assistance. A research team in Paris may pose a question to the community. The answer is hidden in the mind of a colleague in Bangalore.

It's 11:45 on Sunday night, and you are putting the final touches on a presentation you'll deliver Monday morning to the chief operating officer and his team. One key point you want to emphasize is that the new procurement process still has some rough spots that are hindering productivity. To find some specific data, you go to the corporate discussion forum and search on "procurement." Instantly you have at hand twenty-four different discussion threads that were started since the implementation of the new procurement process. Six of these forums deal with specific problems. You are able to review these forums to capture the most pressing concerns of employees across the globe. In addition to the summary you provide, you also capture a few quotes that adeptly describe the critical issues. You have a more accurate and current view of key organizational issues through this source...and you've done all this at 11:45 in the evening!

Another common use for discussion forums inside organizations is to reduce the load on help desk resources. Rather than calling the helpdesk or logging an online service ticket, employees can look to a discussion forum to help troubleshoot issues for each other. They often discover workarounds and fixes to common problems, and forums serve as a way to share those frequent questions and answers with the next frustrated employee. Forums are particularly geared toward affinity groups or communities of practice. For example, the quality group may have its own forum to share best practices in measurement; the product development group may use the forum as a central place to share competitive information or to check on the status of the development process for any new product release. Central to the success of these forums is the kindred spirit of the community. Discussion forums are a great way for employees to become energized by their collaborative workplace, to feel that they are part of a single larger community, and to know that their additions to the forums are useful to others. The threaded discussion also allows them see a conversation unfold between team members who were previously strangers to each other, but who share a common experience in the company.

Corporate discussion forums also play a valuable role in learning and development strategies. A provocative question can be posed to a group of learners, and the resulting threads provide an opportunity for ideas to build on each other and for the learners to learn from each other. Turn that scenario around: employees can pose provocative questions or ideas regarding strategic direction to executive leadership. The resulting "conversation" between executives and employees is not only genuine and authentic, but it has the potential to bring both groups closer together.

Microblog

Plain and simple: a "mini blog" consisting of 140 characters or less (the maximum visible on cell phone screens) that answers the basic question "What are you doing?" This message goes to the cell phones or computers of those who choose to receive your updates.

There are a few primary microblogging sites: Plurk, Jaiku, and Twitter. The larger social networking sites (Facebook, MySpace, LinkedIn, and XING) also provide a form of microblogging, though it's frequently called a *status update* on these sites. Perhaps the most notable microblogging tool at the time of this writing is Twitter. Despite being one of the newer technologies to hit the social media scene, its use is growing exponentially. It sprung up within the San Francisco–based podcasting company Odeo in 2006. Jack Dorsey had an itch to keep in better touch with his friends; he wondered what they were up to. To satisfy his itch, Dorsey created Twitter as a research and development project, and it quickly became an internal tool for Odeo employees. In August 2006 it was launched publicly with Dorsey's new company, Obvious, and it blossomed as a tool for the early adopter crowd. It turns out that the itch was contagious, and it seemed that everybody wanted to keep in touch with his or her friends' latest activities. In May 2007, Twitter Incorporated was founded, and the itch has since become viral. In September 2008, comScore reported there were 5.57 million visitors to Twitter,[13] an increase of nearly five times the number of visitors from the previous year, and now politicians, including the governor of California, are using it to communicate.

Twitter enables users to keep in touch with their friends or with others whom they find interesting. Each blast of 140 characters or less is called a tweet. Users can search for particular people and choose to "follow them" by receiving their tweets either on their cell phones or at their computers. Many people scratch their heads in bewilderment when they first learn of Twitter. At first glance it seems a trivial activity, but its power rests in its short flash of useful information. You share resources with those who have purposefully signed up to hear what you have to say, and you have opted to receive news from people who are likely to say things that you know you'll want to hear. Imagine that you are at a professional conference and have just heard an amazing speaker with a fascinating new book. You send a tweet out to your followers: "At the International Leadership conference. Great speaker on social media inside organizations. Fascinating book: Social Media at Work." Instantly they get the word on a topic that is likely to be of interest to most of them.

Organizations are starting to see the value of microblogging. At Zappos, 435 of its 1,300 employees are on Twitter. CEO Tony Hsieh has the esteemed designation of "Twitter Rank: #1," with 800,000 followers. He is a huge fan of this social networking tool. Revealing his perspective, he says, "It's going to seem a little weird at first, but I promise you if you can talk your friends into joining it and you all use it for 2 weeks, it will change your life. You will wonder how you ever lived without it."[14] And, as you can guess, it's a great way to build a culture within your company while building a loyal and engaged customer base as well.

Inside the organization. Many organizations are discovering the value of a microblog's capability. IBM has been exploring a number of social networking technologies, and Blue Twit is its Twitter-based solution. With more than four hundred thousand employees across the globe, IBM realizes that the days of popping into someone's office for a quick chat are over. It is impossible for colleagues working on a difficult problem to grab a cup of coffee and a fresh perspective in the cafeteria. And they won't share stories about their kids' great pass or piano recital in the parking lot. Instead, they must get to know each other in ways that compensate for the loss of face time. IBM believes that Blue Twit is one way to do this.[15]

Imagine the possibilities when trying to build rapport and relationships on new virtual teams. Twitter is a quick, easy way to bridge the oceans and allow people a much better glimpse of how their colleagues in other time zones and cultures (as well as those in the home office next door) live, what makes them tick, and what matters to them. That better understanding helps everyone work more effectively together.

The power of microblogging also lies in its ubiquitousness. Team members can communicate key ideas with each other no matter where they are or what they're doing. Whether members are on the train commuting to work, standing in line in a coffee shop, or watching a son's football game, these moments are ripe for a flash of brilliance, a new twist, a grand insight that could be shared with the others in real time. The flurry of tweets in response could take the team in an entirely new direction.

Podcast

Plain and simple: a series of downloadable audio sessions that are sent to subscribers on demand for play on their computers or their mobile mp3 players.

Podcasts are audio files that are recorded and uploaded to an Internet server. The creator, the podcaster, can use a variety of recording tools to create an mp3 or .wav file. One of the most popular is Audacity, a free, downloadable application that allows you to record yourself and creates mp3 files as an output. Once the file is created, it is uploaded to a server and available through a variety of Internet blogging and Web site developer tools. But the sweet spot about podcasting is the ability to syndicate the file and make it available to subscribers. Andrea is a typical podcast subscriber. Oprah Winfrey has made it easy for her to ask for one of Oprah's podcast series. She simply went to Oprah's podcast site and clicked on the "Podcast on iTunes" link. Her iTunes application automatically launched and presented her with the link to confirm her subscription. Now she will see a new podcast in her iTunes library every Tuesday, ready for her to watch on her computer or download for that day's bike ride.

This is a key benefit of podcasts: convenience. What a great way to multitask when you're unable to do much else—while slogging through a long commute, working in the yard, knitting a sweater, painting the bedroom.

Inside the organization. Podcasts are a whole new medium for communicating in organizations and have numerous applications. The possibilities are perhaps most obvious in learning and development. Generation Y is quite comfortable accepting an assignment to download and listen to a mini lecture that augments the classroom experience.

In small businesses, nonprofits, and volunteer groups, podcasts are a great way for leaders to share their latest strategy, the company's recent sales success, or new regulations that affect employee decisions. In large organizations, podcasts are most useful to global organizations with a mobile employee base. These employees have become quite accustomed to downloading on the go. As a sales rep, Jessica needs to know her prospect well before she shakes anyone's hand. While she flies, she listens to her company's standard profile on this prospect; the news feed she subscribes to regarding her prospect's company; and the previous sales rep's audio file describing the sales call, personalities, and needs of the key decision makers. By the time the flaps go up, Jessica is ready.

At Oracle, podcasts are used as educational offerings in a variety of groups. Team members subscribe to a podcast, and as new recordings are made, they are fed directly to the employees. Salespeople can get updates on product features, leaders can hear the latest thought leaders in their industry, and teams can share podcasts with each other. One group even used a podcast in its strategic planning process. At an off-site, the team split into three smaller groups and donned their individual mp3 players. Each group took a different walking path and were instructed to pause at key landmarks. "This is stop number two. Notice how the tree trunk wraps itself around the boulder as if intertwined. We enjoy a great relationship with our external partners. In the coming year, how can we partner more effectively with them so that our efforts are intertwined and dovetail most effectively? When you're ready, turn the recording off, share ideas with your team, and capture your most important thoughts for the meeting." Upon their return, the groups shared their responses to the same planning questions, but each had a different landmark to trigger their discussion. Each team shared a unique and memorable experience, rich small-group discussions, the adventure of an unknown trail, and a great opportunity for team building.

Web Conferencing

Plain and simple: a conference for people who are in different locations that enables them to see the same computer screen on their individual computers and be in a live conversation together over a phone or VOIP line.

Web conferencing came on the scene in the late 1990s and has gained many add-on capabilities since then. Common features include the ability to poll the participants on a question, receive instant results, and share them with everyone. Presenters can grant shared control or turn over full control to another participant at any time, so that the group benefits from the collective hard drive of the entire team. A chat feature enables team members to have small side conversations to ask questions or make comments to individuals or to the entire group.

Inside the organization. Today, web conferencing is commonplace in many larger corporations. Often, it is the way teams hold their meetings, collaborate on documents, and make decisions together. Because each team member is able to see the computer screen of the presenter, team members can have a meeting as though they were sitting around a table with a handout, the old-fashioned way. Unlike a videoconference that requires participants in different locations to be at a site with special equipment, web conferencing allows them to be anywhere in the world and still be together. All they need is their Internet connection. Three common web conferencing tools are Webex, GoToMeeting, and Live Meeting. Some companies, such as Oracle, have even developed their own solutions.

Virtual World

Plain and simple: a simulated environment on the Web where anyone can live an imaginary life—take on a new identity, create a business, buy, sell, meet people, and just hang out.

Baby Boomers had the movie *West World*; Gen X, *Total Recall*; and Gen Y, *The Matrix*—stories of regular people caught in a parallel existence. Unlike the film characters trapped in the scenarios portrayed by those movies, people today *choose* to live in virtual worlds. You too can live in a real-time, parallel life that exists only in the ether. Virtual worlds include Entropia Universe, There, and Active Worlds, but probably the most commonly used virtual world is Second Life (SL). "Avatar," "Linden dollar," and the "Grid"—these are some of the terms you'll learn as a new member of the SL tribe. An avatar is a computer-simulated representation of a person, a Linden dollar is SL's unit of currency, and Grid refers to the networked collection of SL servers that create, for example, the virtual world's representation of land.

If you don't like who you've turned out to be in real life, if you've wanted to test out a new small business model, or if you're holding a party for two hundred other alter-personas whom you've never met, SL is the place to be. Created by Linden Labs in June 2003, SL has become a staple among a relatively small but growing group of ardent fans. As of September 2008, slightly more than fifteen million accounts were registered on SL. Approximately thirty-eight thousand residents were logged on and "inworld" at any given time.

Inside the organization. Virtual worlds have many uses for organizations, particularly in the learning environment. They offer a perfect simulated environment, helping employees play out their roles and experiment without hurting sales or customer service. In SL, any organization can become a resident. A small sample of familiar companies who are in SL includes BMW, Sony, Vodafone, Virgin, Reuters, Reebok, and ABC TV. Virtual worlds provide organizations countless applications for learning and development, product development, market research, and sales. Organizations can hold global meetings in virtual worlds and can invite other teams or partners to join them. They can host the meeting in a custom-created environment, complete with decorations that express their company culture. Product developers can play out scenarios, test user opinion, and build prototypes. You should note that SL's terms of service stipulate that all residents retain copyright to their own intellectual property, which makes this a relatively safe place to experiment on business models, new products, and so on.

Virtual worlds have also caught on in higher education institutions. For example, Eduserv found that 80 percent of UK universities had some form of teaching or learning activities on SL.[16] One island in the grid, Scilands, is entirely devoted to science and technology education, and hosts a variety of organizations, including the Spaceflight Museum, NASA, the National Institutes of Health, and Jet Propulsion Laboratory.

One clear organizational application is to use virtual worlds as the next generation of web conferencing. Imagine that your globally dispersed team convenes a meeting—in the grid, of course—at a resort (owned and operated by a wealthy hotelier avatar . . . perhaps your real-life next-door neighbor, the electrician). The team of avatars sit around a large conference table, share issues, show video clips, engage in heated debate, revise documents, and make decisions . . . all before 4:00 P.M., when everyone moves to the tiki bar for some socializing with other executives who have convened at the same resort. Not a bad way to cut down on travel expenses!

As we can see from the diversity and novelty of tools described here, the depth and breadth of social media's utility within organizations is rapidly expanding. Although we have explored what many consider to be the major types of social media currently available, scores of other tools and platforms also exist—new ones are under constant development. Each tool we've mentioned has a plethora of applications within organizations, whether in enhancing learning and development, advancing innovation, or increasing employee engagement. So how do we organize all the social content generated by this media? Let's discuss this next.

Shortcuts for Efficiency: Tagging and RSS Feeds

The entrepreneurial spirit and continuous advances in technology keep all of us inundated with new sites, new tools, and new gadgets. It can surely be overwhelming at times. Although we could cover many other social technologies, two useful tools deserve particular attention because they help us receive more value from our social media by making the information accessible when we need it the most. Tagging and RSS feeds must have been created by those who needed a tidy desk and who always knew where they left their keys. On behalf of the rest of us, thank you!

Tagging

Plain and simple: assigning a piece of information a keyword that will help you find it again later.

In 2004, Robert was working on his final term paper in Spanish history. He had spent hours scouring the Internet for information and printing pages. He had attached a sticky note to the front page of each article he had collected, labeling it with the key topics he needed to reference. He had separated the articles according to his labels. The fruits of his labor had spread across his dormitory room floor in six neat stacks of paper: Phoenicians, Moors, Inquisition, Bourbons, Franco, Democracy.

Today, Robert's task is much easier, thanks to the system called tagging. Known as *metadata,* tags are keywords that we assign to bits of Internet information to categorize them for later use. A collection of tags is called a folksonomy, as opposed to a taxonomy. The difference is subtle but important.

Taxonomies are like the file folders or bookmarking structures found on our computer hard drives. In a common (hierarchical) taxonomy, a particular document or piece of information is usually filed or stored in "one best place." When you want to find it later, you had better hope you've "filed" it correctly.

In contrast, a folksonomy is a bottom-up structure. The user tags each bit of information with a label or many labels. There is no right or wrong, and there is no limit to the number of tags a bit of information may have. This way, the user can search by the keywords that have meaning for him to find the information (Web page) that fits his need. A content creator who wants her information to get into the right hands will tag her blog, article, or Web site with the most appropriate keywords.

Delicious.com is a social bookmarking utility that enables users to bookmark a Web site and add a tag to the bookmark to help in finding it later. Delicious will suggest existing tags as you begin typing so that you don't inadvertently create two versions of the same tag ("tool" and "tools"). Delicious further allows you to organize tags by bundling them together into tag "clouds."

The *social* part of Delicious is the unique feature of bookmark sharing. In 2009, as Robert is working on his doctoral thesis on Spanish emigration, he has more than twenty-two hundred bookmarks in nineteen tag clouds in his Delicious account. He learns that his cousin is writing her thesis on Hawaii's immigrant populations at the turn of the century. Because so many Spaniards went to Hawaii to pick sugar cane in the early 1900s, he quickly sends her his bookmarks tagged with "Hawaii" and "ships." She instantly has access to his hard-earned research, and she'll return the favor by sending Robert her bookmarks tagged with "Iberia."

Delicious may have been the forerunner, but many social technologies have added this valuable feature to their services.

Some sort of tagging feature exists in Flickr (a photo sharing tool), Technorati (a search engine), Digg (a Web content sharing and ranking tool), and in the big three—blogs, wikis, and social networking sites.

RSS Feed

Plain and simple: a request to have updated Web sites (blog, wiki, news article, and so on) sent directly to you as the updates occur.

Really Simple Syndication (RSS) is a way for Web site creators to alert their readers when they have revised the content of their Web site. They use an RSS feeder to offer their Web site to be scanned regularly by those who want to follow their changes. This assures them that their audience will be aware of the important message they want to convey on their site.

Because most of us are on the "receiving end" of the Internet, we can think of it as a research assistant who gathers today's news and puts it on our desk. If Carl wants to follow the news from his top three competitors and a blog written by a particular marketing expert, he can make this task easier with RSS feeds. Rather than checking each of those Web sites every day, Carl simply clicks on the RSS icon on each of these Web sites. An RSS aggregator is like his assistant. Each day it scans the sites that he has requested, and if any changes have been made on the site, the aggregator lists them for Carl in one place—typically his Yahoo or Google personal home page. It's as though he has his own online newspaper and has asked his assistant to gather any breaking news on these particular topics only and to create a customized front page of the headlines.

Obviously, the RSS feed is a valuable tool, no matter which side of the Internet you're on. If you have a message to convey and you want to make it more readily available to those who are interested, you create an RSS feed on your Web site. If you're a user who is interested in keeping abreast of changes on a variety of sites, setting up your RSS reader is an indispensable resource—the most affordable assistant you'll ever have.

Weaving a Tapestry

The lines are blurring between different social media because they can be combined, embedded, and intertwined. A simple example of this is a video or audio clip embedded in a wiki. It is possible to post pictures on any social networking site. In fact, many social technology tools allow you to use combinations of a variety of social media.

For example, Voicethread is a tool that allows you to post an image and invite commentary from the community. Individuals can comment by recording their voice, typing a comment, or sharing a video comment. To add the social networking component, each participant's photo and profile are added as she responds. In addition, participants can jot notes on a notepad or use a whiteboard marker to point at, circle, or color images. The resulting "conversation" is saved along the way and can be played back and added to later. One can imagine the usefulness for architects designing a groundbreaking building or for fashion designers creating their fall collection.

A more elaborate example is commonly referred to as a *mashup*, an integration of different data sources into one Web site. Creating a mashup is more complex than simply embedding different media, in that the creator grabs third-party data using an application programming interface tool. Mashups serve to repurpose the data and present it to the user in a uniquely useful way to serve the purpose of the Web site.

In either case, the tapestry is rich with color and texture. In today's social networking efforts, organizations can weave together all sorts of social media to serve their needs. One example of an organization using a wide variety of social media is Oracle Corporation.

Trailblazer—Social Media at Oracle

As the world's leading business software company, Oracle Corporation has no shortage of tech-savvy employees. Exploring how new technologies can improve business performance is what they're all about, and they are experiencing the same opportunities as many other companies by using social media in a variety of ways.

TRAILBLAZER

The post came up on Steve's screen: "Will this social network help us in our daily jobs?" A member of Oracle's Consulting Services, Steve thought about it and felt compelled to answer, "I think yes. Oracle Connect has the potential to help us with our daily jobs, especially if it is expanded beyond just a Groups / Ideas / Blogs / Questions tool into a complete Social Publishing utility that includes Wiki, and Content Management, archiving etc. I believe a combined solution is essential for efficient Knowledge Management in our organisation."

When Jake saw that response, he had to chime in: "That's our goal!" As the product strategy director, Jake Kuramoto knows all about Oracle Connect, the internal social networking utility for employees. Oracle Connect began as a grassroots experiment and grew to be a widespread tool for collaborating and connecting people and information within Oracle. The work environment at Oracle is a fast-paced one based on innovation and technology. The company has a culture of "self-service," and employees use technology wherever possible to improve quality or efficiency. But with so much information and so many options, people can sometimes struggle to find the right information at the time they need it. Oracle Connect is a key tool to put that information at their fingertips. Employees can see a full profile of their colleagues to better understand their respective roles. Employees thereby gain a wealth of knowledge about each other, including skills, personalities, and backgrounds. Employees can create or join interest groups (for example, diversity networks), post questions or answers ("What feedback do you have on the new data finder tool?"), send e-mail, or propose an idea by clicking on the ever-present "Got an idea? Share it!" button.

Oracle Connect is just one way Oracle uses social media to help employees become more effective. The company also uses discussion forums, wikis, microblogging, and a variety of community portals to connect people and ideas. Social networking is coming through clearly in Oracle's applications as well. Because the company uses its own applications internally, it has a great stake in their usefulness. The new versions of Oracle's talent management applications include data-rich employee profiles that will assist with talent development processes, resource allocation, and succession planning. Leaders will have a different view of the capabilities of their organization and will be better equipped to make smart decisions for their employees and the business.

Making better decisions is the goal behind the proliferation of wikis, blogs, and discussion forums at Oracle. The O Direct Blog site has thousands of blog posts on a wide variety of topics. As of this writing, over two thousand blogs have been initiated in the "applications" category. The top blogger has 983 posts. This site enables employees to search, sort by date and popularity, subscribe to a blog, and access podcasts and videos. Employees share opinions and ideas on just about everything that can help them become more effective. In fact, Oracle's microblogging tool, Oratweet, was first piloted by the Fusion Talent Management product group to help bridge communication gaps and speed decisions within their distributed team. "We needed a sort of virtual war room," said Mark Bennett, director in the product strategy group. But that's not the only place microblogging adds value. Oracle recruiter David Talamelli is ranked thirty-five among the top fifty users on Twitter.[17] Recruiters have found Twitter to be a great way to keep close to future employees.

TRAILBLAZER

Discussion forums have emerged as a valuable way for employees to help each other. The MyOracleForums page has thousands of messages. For example, the thread titled "How to render an HTML dashboard in Excel spreadsheet to a presentation page?" received several quick answers. Imagine the time and resource savings gained when these questions are asked and answered within minutes. A different use of forums is found in the Oracle Women's Leadership program (OWL). This community of women leaders has its own OWL portal, which houses resources for women, leadership development opportunities, news and research, and a robust discussion forum highlighting executive women writing about timely issues. This internal social networking site has been a fantastic way for women to share ideas, learn from others, and build useful relationships. Patricia Cureton, cofounder of OWL, believes that providing women leaders the ability to engage as a community is one of the best ways to retain these valuable employees.

Another way Oracle endeavors to retain its top talent is by providing them ways to innovate and collaborate more effectively. Employees in nearly every line of business use wikis to move projects forward and share ideas and key documents. In one example, the Global Organization and Talent Development (OTD) group uses a wiki as a work space for each of its global projects. Although Oracle teams are comfortable working across time zones, it is still difficult to evoke the best from every team member when someone in California is thinking at 5:00 A.M., and someone in Beijing is thinking at 11:00 P.M. The OTD group found that using the wiki as the primary gathering place to house strategic decisions, project plans, and resources worked well as a way for team members to contribute during the time they can be most productive. The Leadership Development Center of Excellence, a global team of internal leadership development practitioners, created its vision, strategic plan, and project plan by posting these documents on the wiki and asking team members to improve on them.

Using social media isn't always a walk in the park. Like many other large organizations, Oracle struggles to maintain a balance between allowing employees to take independent action and needing to find consistent tools to make access easier, reduce learning curves, and find the best leverage. Issues of appropriate usage have and will continue to occur. In addition, with so many options for communicating and collaborating, employees can find it difficult to know which tool—the wiki, the forum, or Oracle Connect—will be the best venue for interaction. Still, the viral reach gained from any one of these tools can prove much more valuable than that of an e-mail sent to a limited and known set of colleagues. As Oracle has discovered, the collective wisdom of many individuals collaborating together inevitably surpasses the contribution of the best personal acquaintance alone.

Your Toolbox Is Stocked

In this chapter, we have opened up a treasure chest of terms and concepts in the language of social media. We have introduced just a few of the key tools available to us all and a way to understand their uses in a variety of organizational settings. As we've discussed, attempting to provide an exhaustive list would be futile, as technologies continue to advance and collaborative communities devise tools useful to both broad audiences and niche groups. A common question is, "Which tool should I use?" Of course the annoying answer is, "It depends." As we've seen, your decision depends on the audience, their perspective, and their willingness to use various tools. It also depends on your objectives and goals. Are you mostly trying to communicate (likely a blog), collaborate (likely a wiki), or connect (likely a social networking site)? Notwithstanding, we hope that we've helped equip you with at least a rudimentary understanding of social media and that you can imagine some uses for these tools in your organization. In the next chapter, we'll share examples of where we've seen social media offer some of the greatest benefits to organizations. We're confident that like our friend Lana from the beginning of this chapter, none of us will have to speak any longer in low tones and a hushed voice when discussing the wonderful world of Web 2.0.

Join the Conversation

Connect with others who, like you, are exploring, experimenting, and pioneering the use of social media to propel organizational performance. Go to www.socialmediaatwork-connection.com to ask your questions, learn what others are doing, and add your insights to the conversation. This chapter raises the following questions for you and your fellow community members:

- What are the most common social media tools you are using?
- How can you combine social media in new ways to add value to your organization?
- What questions do you have that others might also want to ask?

4

WHERE SOCIAL MEDIA HAS AN IMPACT

Catherine hung up the phone, locked her computer screen, and slid her chair away from her desk. She grabbed her purse and headed down the hall to meet her friends for lunch. She had just completed a two-hour live webinar, and was excited about the information she had received and the homework she would complete with two colleagues, one in her office in Galway, Ireland, and another located outside of London, England. They were all members of Cisco's Development Organization (CDO), and they were learning about the latest social computing technologies. This was the second of four two-hour webinars that Catherine and her colleagues would participate in over the course of four months. She loved the exchanges that always ensued as her Western Europe colleagues shared their questions and ideas.

Cisco, the worldwide leader in networking software, hardware, and services, has been using social media to create customized learning solutions for their employees. As a large, fast-moving global company with employees dispersed across the globe, it is a challenge and a business imperative to enable employees to continually refresh their skills. Social computing technologies have played a key role in employee development. Web 2.0 and collaboration are woven into the fabric of Cisco's learning and development culture, and Cisco sees its use as a model of running a sustainable business.

Social media has been utilized in learning and development at Cisco for four primary reasons. First, it is part of the company's corporate culture and critical to its strategy. CEO John Chambers has encouraged the use of these new technologies with a focus on collaborating and connecting with customers, partners, employees, and communities. With Web 1.0, Cisco claimed to be the first company to do support, case management, and orders online. Web 2.0 is viewed as a market transition, impacting the way businesses are run. Cisco desires to be at the forefront of this transition and is heavily investing in making it happen smoothly. Greg Brower leads Cisco's curriculum planning and deployment in the Cisco Development Organization (CDO). His group is responsible for enabling the learning and development of approximately 40 percent of Cisco's key talent. Among them are the software and hardware design engineers. He explains, "We are there to partner with the business units to identify high value opportunities, try it, shake it out, and use it to effectively run the business."

Second, social media is cost effective. The smart use of social media helps to cut expenses and reduce the opportunity cost associated with travel for traditional instructor-led training. Through social media, experts have access to more affordable ways to design learning experiences.

Third, social media scales more effectively to meet a global audience's training needs. In the past, instructors flew across the world for face-to-face training in small groups. With social technologies, time zone boundaries are no longer a barrier to sharing complex knowledge with huge groups of distributed employees. Through CDO's "Nerd Lunch" program, the company routinely uses telepresence technology to enable the technical transfer of information from

Austin, Texas, to large audiences in San Jose, California, and beyond.

Fourth, social media engages employees in sharing knowledge and expertise. Says Greg Brower: "We believe that the more engaged the employees are, the more satisfied and productive they will be. For CDO, it's about enabling engineers to share the very thing that makes them come to work—knowledge and innovation. Engagement is a smart thing to do, and Web 2.0 is a critical way to do it." Brower's comments echo the support that social media has at Cisco, far beyond its learning solutions.

The course that Cisco's pursuing has resulted in a plethora of creative design, development, and delivery techniques using social media technology. Cisco's CDO group incorporates Web 2.0 into their solutions, learning as much as possible about social computing to ensure that it can stay ahead of the competition. When traditional instructor-led training failed to meet the organization's requirements for low-cost speed of deployment to a global audience, CDO's technology executives approached Brower's Curriculum Team, challenging it to find a way to incorporate Web 2.0 technologies into its curriculum development process.

In partnership with the voice technology group, the curriculum team came through with an exemplary approach. A wiki was used to gather training requirements and create a proposal for executives. The actual curriculum design was completed through a wiki as well with contributions from subject matter experts on discussion forums, video links, and question-and-answer dialogues using WebEx virtual conferences. In essence, the curriculum design process became a structured conversation using Web 2.0 tools. In this manner, the team was able to quickly and effectively share project information, identify training requirements, design an effective solution, and make their executive proposal.

TRAILBLAZER

Catherine, our collaborator at the beginning of this story, has a course that is one component of the training solution. Her curriculum team agreed to build four two-hour sessions of Web 2.0 training delivered completely virtually using WebEx technology. The schedule was designed in a way that enabled the sessions to happen during local business hours so that Catherine and her colleagues in Western Europe could participate together, while colleagues in China and India could participate together.

In creating these sessions, the design team never met face-to-face, nor did they know each other prior to this effort. All of their meetings, drafts, prototypes, and final solutions were a result of virtual collaboration.

Of course, the project was not without its challenges along the way. As the first project of its kind, it required much learning and adjusting. The wiki helped tremendously in this process. Each time a module was delivered, the session could be improved because of the collaboration that occurred via the wiki and conference calls. Another challenge centered on the technology capabilities and infrastructure required to support Web 2.0 applications. At the beginning of the project the executives were engaged, understood the risks, and were ready to push the organization toward new and different ways of training. When the designers used WebEx (a Cisco product) with streaming video, the session did not go as smoothly as planned and the facilitators had to improvise. The executives became aware of this "bump" in the process and highlighted it as something that the trainers should avoid in the future. The lesson was noted: facilitators, technology, and infrastructure all need to be ready for prime time to retain credibility for everyone involved. In sessions going forward, capabilities of the technology were well tested prior to going live with any learning experience.

At any rate, through the use of social media, the entire Cisco organization received a full day of technical training and exposure to various Web 2.0 tools, a win-win situation. Employees learned about social technologies by using them in their training, and Cisco experienced significant cost savings on education delivery—a 90 percent reduction in training costs per attendee. With nearly 2,500 attendees in this one training session alone, the savings were substantial. Not to mention, with the reduction in attendee travel expenses, the learning solution also aligned with Cisco's corporate social responsibility goals for reducing carbon emissions. The collaboration and partnership that resulted through this experience reinforced a move that Cisco is making away from hierarchical (command-and-control) management to a more collaborative leadership philosophy.

Equally important, the training raised the awareness of social computing technologies as enablers, a conversation that has been transformational for the organization. As CDO's chief technology officer indicated, the engineers now gained competencies, which were subsequently assessed with quizzes that showed over a 97 percent training completion rate. The use of Web 2.0 technologies was supported and sponsored by the CEO and senior officers of Cisco, and it fostered stronger partnership and collaboration between organizations. The resulting trust needed for long-term effectiveness within these organizations was considered one of the biggest wins of all.

TRAILBLAZER

Capitalizing on Organizational Benefits

Cisco is not alone in its leading-edge use of social media. We have been fortunate to talk to many organizations that are trailblazers in this exciting era. Intel, British Telecom, Emergent Solutions, and many others from a variety of industries are exploring the ways in which they can leverage the new people power that social media technologies make possible. In our many conversations with these eager organizations, we've seen at least five specific areas where they are capitalizing on social media to make a real difference:

1. Attracting and retaining the best employees
2. Innovation and knowledge creation
3. Operational efficiency
4. Talent development
5. Employee engagement

When increased communication, stronger connections, and greater collaboration are added to an organization's daily operations, each of these areas becomes a force that can improve organizational performance and effectiveness. Collectively they influence many key aspects of an organization, such as strategic planning, organization design, change management, leadership development, performance management, and diversity. This is especially true if we view the organization as a system that exists within a larger system.

It is evident in today's volatile economy that companies cannot survive in the long term without attending to more than just quotas and quarterly profit. Enron, WorldCom, AIG, and Lehman Brothers are perfect examples of organizations that, among other things, disregarded the long-term view, the systemic nature of their own workforce dynamics, and the environment beyond their own walls. Obviously, this myopic view can be fatal.

Many would expect greater innovation and knowledge as well as operational efficiencies to contribute to a company's short-term or more immediate success. We agree. However, we also see these forces interacting with the other three organizational elements already mentioned. Attracting and retaining the best employees, talent development, and employee engagement are activities that create the kind of committed organization that can sustain its success and meet the challenges of the future. Each of these five forces strengthens the other in a continuous reinforcing system. They are interdependent and often intertwined.

An organization must not only secure the best resources but also retain them. It is widely recognized that the best predictors of retention are employee satisfaction, commitment, and engagement.[1] The work must be continually engaging. Opportunities for learning and skill development are imperative for the younger employee eager to make a contribution. Truly engaged employees tend to be more productive and have lower turnover than employees who are disengaged. Once engaged, employees naturally seek more ways to create together. They will find innovative methods of streamlining outdated processes and accelerating their time to design, produce, and market their products and services.

However, developing an engaged workforce isn't as easy as it sounds. Nearly one in five employees feels disconnected from work, and voluntary turnover is influenced tremendously by social affiliation both within and outside the organization.[2] To attain these higher levels of productivity and meet customer needs, it is essential to focus on strategies that encourage employee participation and involvement.[3] That's where social media can contribute most—enabling energized employees to connect ideas and collaborate in ways that were previously impossible.

Simply stated, if an organization can attract the best candidates, develop their skills, and provide them opportunities to innovate and gain knowledge, employees will find ways to make their work more productive and efficient, leading to greater employee engagement, retention, and positive results. In this fortunate scenario, an organization retains not only its workforce over time but also sustained performance. Although it is difficult to tease the contributing elements apart, we will try to distinguish them so that we can illuminate opportunities to inject into them the advantages of social media. We offer an overview of these elements in this chapter and explore how social media is strengthening the impact employees can have on the organization. In the next chapter, we will share even more stories representative of each area discussed here.

Attracting and Retaining the Best Employees

Laurie Buczek, Intel's social computing program manager, describes her observations of recruiting the Millennial employee:

> The face of our workforce is dramatically changing. We have the four generations here, and they're very different in how they use technology to connect in their everyday environment. The younger generation is expecting that social media tools are available to them. They don't know any other world; they are totally wired in multiple fashions at the same time. They expect to find this in the work environment, and if we don't provide that for them here, they very quickly disengage and leave for other companies that are providing that robust connection. Word spreads fast among them, and that hinders our ability to attract them in the first place.

Intel knows the profile of the new hires it seeks, both younger and older. Let's review a few characteristics of the members of Gen Y entering the workforce. Penelope Trunk is the CEO of the Brazen Careerist, a Web service that helps connect companies with candidates and helps candidates navigate a successful career. Describing herself as a "Gen Xer—part of the most disenfranchised, neglected generation in history," Trunk shares information that allows both companies and Gen Y job seekers to understand each other and mutually succeed. Trunk notes that the Millennial generation views the employment experience differently than previous generations. Because they work to live, rather than live to work, they view a job as an experience that should continuously afford them an opportunity to contribute, learn new skills, and enjoy working in teams. If their current role should grow stale in these areas, they are more apt to leave and seek a more vibrant role. Consequently, they expect that the relationship with the company may be shorter, or may exist in waves during which they work, leave, and possibly return at a later date for a new and rewarding assignment—and they're OK with that.[4]

So finding the right candidates and enticing them to select your organization will be competitive business in this war for talent. Many of the primary weapons of choice include social networking sites, blogging, and microblogging. Salesforce.com, a software company that sells customer relationship management solutions, recognizes that the Gen X and Gen Y workforce it is targeting will constitute 60 percent of the workforce. The company views the use of social networking sites as a critical recruiting tool. In Chapter Five, we'll learn about the recruiting efforts of Salesforce.com and how it's using social media to reach the right candidates.

Trunk of Brazen Careerist emphasizes the best ways to use corporate blogs to attract the right candidates. Conversations abound in cyberspace about companies—the work they do and their corporate personality and ethos. A corporate blog serves as a way for the company to be part of the conversation, guiding perception and steering the conversation to topics it believes should be discussed. Twitter is emerging as a "must-have" tool for younger candidates entering the workforce and for savvy employers who want to capture them. Hire Strategies, Ltd., a UK-based consultancy dedicated to helping employers use social media to hire, develop, and retain the best employees, featured a blog post focusing on seven reasons that employers should be "twittercruiting," citing free advertising for the company, the addition of the human touch for intimidated candidates, and the vast networking advantages. It also noted a very practical return on time and investment, emphasizing the high yield that a quick and simple tweet can produce.[5]

Once you hire these prime candidates, you must acclimate them to your organization as effectively as possible and allow them to become productive as quickly as possible. Aside from having their desk, phone, and Internet connection ready on day one, it is vital to connect them with a network of colleagues that can help them assimilate quickly into the company and culture. Imagine the need for such a network in a company like Humana that relies heavily on its relationships to accomplish work. New hires turn to internal social networking sites to gain awareness of who's who, who can help them with their assignment, and whom they can help as well. In fact, many college hires are beginning to expect this as part of the on-boarding process when matriculating into companies.

The changing career life cycle mentioned earlier, coupled with the increasing diversity in all organizations, are two drivers for organizations to build effective bridges—connecting the knowledge, wisdom, and fresh ideas of multiple generations, as well as the frames of reference embedded in our cultural and demographic backgrounds. These are critical retention factors, and they can foster a desired brand in the marketplace. For example, 26 percent of the external hires at consulting firm Ernst & Young are rehires. Ernst & Young has made it clear that rehires are welcome and valued. They are 50 percent less expensive to recruit, come up to speed twice as fast, and are 40 percent more likely to become top performers. In Chapter Two we saw how Dow Chemical recently launched a social network (My Dow Network) with the goal of linking employees, alumni, and retirees to the company and enabling knowledge transfer to occur. Retirees actually mentor new employees, becoming brand ambassadors, facilitating stronger connections with stakeholders, and preserving the best of the company's cultural heritage.[6]

A variety of women's and other diversity programs are springing up in recognition of the risks associated with losing these experienced segments of the company's human resources. Social media tools play a huge role in connecting those who join these affinity groups and enabling them to interact in new ways. These programs drive retention of valuable employees and improve the appeal of the company in the eyes of the job seeker. In the next chapter, we'll learn how Oracle's OWL program uses social media to connect this powerful community.

Innovation and Knowledge Creation

Gino Creglia Photography is a small, entrepreneurial organization. Creglia has built a very successful photography business by working on catalogue photography, portraiture, and commercial advertising. But the work he enjoys most, and that which has created a loyal customer following, is capturing the moments of everyone's big event: wedding photography. Although business has been good, Creglia has been searching for fresh ideas and inventive services for his business. A good friend told him about social networking sites, and Creglia began to explore. Within three weeks, he had built a community of partner entrepreneurs and redefined his "organization." The members of this new, broader community of complementary businesses continually feed ideas to each other, exchange market information, provide valuable resource connections, and cocreate valuable services for their collective customer base. Creglia notes, "It's like I've expanded my organization with a new creative department, promotion department, and small business support team. The ideas we generate together are much better than anything we had thought of independently. I think we're all energized by our new community and by what we can achieve together. These new social networking tools are fantastic for reaching new customers, but they've been even more valuable *inside* my small shop."

Innovation has been defined many different ways, but all definitions share the elements of creativity and action. There is no such thing as an inventor who harbors all his great ideas silently inside his head. Great ideas need to improve on the status quo and be brought out so that others can make use of them. In our research, we've seen innovation take the form of creative design, product development, and speed in generating results from ideas.[7]

At the heart of great innovation are new knowledge creation, collaboration, the creation of social capital—the advantageous connections between people—and the advent of self-organizing communities. All social media tools enable knowledge creation and social capital, but wikis are the primary tool for collaboration, and social networking sites enable people to find the best collaborators for their efforts.

A pan-European study conducted by Dynamic Markets found that 74 percent of European employees consider the use of social networking sites and online communities in the workplace to be valuable. The two main benefits cited were the tools' ability to increase an individual's knowledge and give access to solutions for problems. Harnessing the collective knowledge of employees, customers, and suppliers, and stimulating team building and better internal collaboration were also mentioned by those employees who use social networks at work on a daily basis.[8]

Picture this scenario: Rami sat in the hot seat, considering each of the four possible answers in front of him. As a guest on the TV game show *Who Wants to Be a Millionaire*, Rami would win $100,000 if he could answer the question correctly. Although he was fairly certain of the correct response, he didn't want to risk such a prize. He went for a "lifeline" and decided to ask the audience for their choice. How many of us would turn over an important decision to a large group of strangers? If you have seen this show, then you know that Rami made a smart choice in asking the audience: they're usually right.

The uncanny accuracy of their collective responses is due to a phenomenon made explicit in James Surowiecki's book, *The Wisdom of Crowds*. Through a wide variety of examples, Surowiecki shows how large numbers of independent people will collectively achieve better results than most individual experts. He describes four conditions that characterize wise crowds: a diversity of perspectives, independence of thought, decentralized specialization (or the ability to tap into local wisdom), and the ability to integrate collective decisions.[9]

Social media tools accelerate the development of this collective wisdom within organizations, enabling this same power of connection among individuals with disparate knowledge. As more knowledge is shared, a new collective wisdom emerges in the organization, and the possibilities for improved ideas, products, and services and more effective business decisions feed each other in a spiraling and cumulative effect.

The nature of this creative process is also reflected in "Open Space Technology" (OST), a method of collaboration that allows for people and ideas to organize themselves as they deem most useful.[10] It's frequently used by organization leaders dealing with urgent business issues that are so complex that no one person can solve them alone without a diversity of insight. The OST philosophy is simple: (1) whoever shows up is the right person, (2) whatever happens is the only thing that could have happened, (3) when it starts, that's the right time, and (4) when it's over, it's over. Open Space fans also espouse a *two feet law*: if you're not contributing or learning, use your two feet and move to where you can. This process is facilitated through the use of such social media tools as wikis, discussion forums, blogs, and social networking sites. As groups and ideas coalesce and self-organize, context is added to the equation.

At Humana, David Woodbury sees the company's social networking efforts as the next generation of the knowledge management strategies of the 1990s. In the past, the structures created to capture knowledge were successful in collecting data, but employees still lacked context for the information. They had a hard time finding the appropriate information and making it useful in a new context. Woodbury sees social networking sites as a huge improvement on this method because a human conduit of information provides the context to apply knowledge to real business problems. "Social networking will be the interface into that depth of knowledge. When I want *information*, I Google it. But when I want *useful knowledge, know-how, or wisdom* from my colleagues, the social network will be indispensable because the people will include the context. Our employees will be able to tap their colleagues' insights while also meeting their fundamental social needs."

Woodbury believes that as Humana becomes more effective in its use of social networks, the company will find a way to enable employees to easily reach out to external sources of innovation. Humana has already recognized a crippling error in assuming that innovation can be fostered only within the company's walls. As a result, it has revised its corporate competency for innovation to encourage leaders to reach out to all their professional and personal networks—internal and external—to further Humana's development of health care solutions. Woodbury explains, "We will expect our leaders and employees to go out and create new networks to tap valuable ideas. This is how we will continue to serve our customers in useful ways."

Operational Efficiency

Organizations are constantly striving to improve their efficiency. Whether it is in incremental improvements or in sweeping changes in their operations, such as business process reengineering, a common mantra that follows "Do it better" is always "and do it faster!" If collaboration for innovation and development lies in the one hand, in the other hand you'll find collaboration to gain efficiency.

The Dynamic Markets survey mentioned earlier included more than twenty-five hundred people in five countries and found that 65 percent of those who responded reported that social networking tools made them or their colleagues more efficient. "The research shows that there is a clear trend across Europe for business users to embrace the benefits of 'Web 2.0' technology to underpin collaboration, improve productivity, and embrace business efficiency."[11] In a SelectMinds survey, employees said that when they used social media to access relevant information quickly, their productivity improved by more than 10 percent.[12]

The ties to the on-boarding process for new employees are clear. The faster that new hires can fit into the culture, find the resources they need, and build relationships that enable them to get things done, the sooner they become an asset for the organization. But existing teams have the same issues. One sales group at Intel discovered that on average, sales reps lose several hours each week searching for the right people and information to be able to best support their customers. The use of social media brings those people and that information to them instantly and allows them to recoup some of the time. At BT Group, employees created an index page on their internal wiki to catalogue the many disparate Web sites holding critical information. In Chapter Five, we'll see more examples of operational efficiencies gained.

Talent Development

At the heart of all great organizations are the *people*. The integration of social media technology into organizations creates myriad opportunities to enhance talent development. Over the past several decades, you have no doubt become familiar with the focus and corresponding human resource development terminology that was most common in each era. Prior to the 1980s, "training" was the topic. In the 1990s, training became "learning," and the broader and more significant potential of "organizational learning" was at the forefront. As we entered the new millennium, "talent development" appeared in corporate documents and trade journals as the contemporary term. This broad descriptor includes such efforts as workforce planning, technical training, leadership development, professional skills development, identification of "high-potentials," talent management, succession planning, and most other activities that involve improving the short- and long-term capability of the members of an organization.

The use of social media lends itself to most activities associated with talent development because it makes information more readily available in all forms, enables people to learn from each other, illuminates tacit or hidden knowledge, and helps extend the learning process over time. It is hard for us to imagine gathering knowledge and learning without the use of Web 2.0 tools. Information is at our fingertips, served up in any number of social media venues: podcasts on sales techniques, wikis to cocreate a class assignment, blogs to share an analysis and opinion of a business decision, and social networking sites that act as an expanded phone directory and information gold mine. The Cisco example shows some of the ways that social media can enable greater scale and cost savings.

Social media also enables members of an organization to learn from each other. No longer are leaders or subject matter experts expected to be the only ones with useful information. Among other tools, discussion forums allow employees to post questions and receive a flood of answers from sources they didn't even know existed. Peer mentoring becomes the norm when anyone can offer a valuable perspective or provide another web of resources to assist with the learning process. And because learning happens best over time, social media can extend the learning time on any development opportunity. In the traditional classroom experience, the instructor shares new information with the participants. But richer learning happens on break when small groups gather around the coffee pot or at the vending machine and conversation breaks out. Community spaces and online portals enable a class or cohort of learners to maintain contact and continue learning well beyond any scheduled event. Members of these communities are often the best sources of learning because they provide just-in-time answers, share similar challenges, and have invested in each other's learning experience. At Oracle, a Global Leadership Academy for senior leaders in its services engineering group enabled thirty participants to make critical business breakthroughs by working together in virtual teams across the globe. The program included a blend of social media and face-to-face sessions as a means of strengthening leadership skills. Through the use of wikis and web conferences, participants identified solutions to three strategic business problems. They built online communities and continued their learning on the job, using their new leadership skills to bring their action learning projects to fruition.

A recent McKinsey Quarterly study shows that 71 percent of organizations surveyed, 1,466 in all, are using Web 2.0 in their training efforts.[13] Many universities have a presence in virtual worlds, enabling students to "meet" at a training center in cyberspace. In June 2009, the International Quality and Performance Center held a conference dedicated to the use of social media for talent management, covering such topics as keeping employees engaged in collaborative learning, creating knowledge resources and sustained communities over the long run, and successfully implementing social media tools into learning solutions.[14]

As noted by Donald Tapscott and others, the capacity of leaders to integrate, leverage, and magnify the talent of diverse (and dispersed) individuals and teams is a key differentiating competency.[15] At Oracle, organization and talent development consultants are beginning to introduce social networking and collaborative forums into leadership development action learning programs in order to spur greater peer dialogue, coaching, and mentoring. Learning and development groups in every kind of organization are likewise incorporating social media into their learning solutions. Cisco, HP, IBM, and Oracle are just a few organizations that are actively using a variety of social media in their talent development efforts.

Employee Engagement

Several years ago, an interesting phenomenon occurred: that of "random acts of kindness." Suddenly people found that their bridge toll had been paid by the person before them. A fresh cup of coffee awaited as you approached the Starbuck's clerk, compliments of the woman who just wished you a good day. And the craze of "pay it forward" inspired people everywhere to do something nice for someone else because . . . well, because it was a good thing to do, and it made the do-gooder feel good too. Similarly, in Amish country, a barn materializes in an open field within two days, thanks to the sweat and determination of an entire community.

Employee engagement is about the basic need for people to be part of something larger than themselves, to contribute in a meaningful way. The power of people inspired to contribute cannot be underestimated. Contribution cannot happen in isolation. It requires connection with others and the exchange that occurs between individuals or between an individual and the group to which he belongs. Engagement drives civilization and society. It fosters innovation and invention. It seals loyal partnerships and affiliations. It catapults careers. In the engagement of hearts, minds, and resources, people have been able to achieve more together than anyone could have achieved alone. The human need for connection and contribution is not new. Our need to affiliate with others is seen in the formation of clans, tribes, and societies. We band together to gain the advantage of collective ideas, expanded resources, leadership vision, and momentum toward the achievement of common goals.

Engagement takes place in every type of organization, and it looks different in each unique situation. Social service organizations find ways to tap the motivation of volunteers and connect them to resources. Entrepreneurs find angel investors and complementary partners. Small businesses grow from shared vision and the energy of inspired contributors. Large corporations enable the emergence of the collaborative genius of their employees across the globe.

Social media tools provide new and powerful ways to engage more of the organization on a wider range of business issues than ever before possible. One global webcast allows all employees to hear a common message. Blogs create visible dialogue and invite independent thought, analysis, and response to a leader's ideas or to any employee's urge to share her opinions. Through wikis and discussion forums, anyone can contribute to an effort that tugs at his passion or pulls on his expertise. Organization leaders can solve complex problems more effectively by simply asking for input and listening to the firestorm of responses from team members. As we noted earlier, the solution that is created from the collective input is often better than the one chosen by a small handful of obvious experts.

But leaders, teams, and individuals gain much more in the process. They build a culture of contribution that capitalizes on the ideas of potentially every employee, allowing them an opportunity to make a difference in large and even small ways. Social media tools enable their input to be seen and heard. This engagement is satisfying and leads to employee retention. In particular, younger generations are determined to engage meaningfully in their jobs. If they are stymied, they will leave in search of an open field and a community that needs their contribution.

Richard Dennison, the senior manager of social media at BT Group, is passionate about using social media to improve engagement at BT. "I firmly believe we really don't get the most from our employees. We put them in narrow, confined spaces, we give them objectives that are limited to one part of the business, and we don't encourage them to contribute more widely."

In this chapter, we've explored how social media technology has emerged as a new tool that organizations can deploy for improved performance in the short and the long term. Some organizations are just becoming aware of the opportunities in using social media internally, but many other organizations are capitalizing on this insight right now. BT Group, formerly known as British Telecom, is one of them. Let's take a closer look at its story to learn of the many ways the company is ahead of the curve.

BT Group: Ahead of the Curve

TRAILBLAZER

In 2007, a young new hire purchased a software server with his corporate credit card and placed it under his desk. The server was a way for him to improve his productivity. Soon Richard Dennison, the senior manager of social media, appeared beside him, not to chastise him for purchasing the equipment through the company, but to share ideas with him and explore ways they could improve productivity for many. That's how it all started at BT Group, the UK-based telecommunications company.

Operating in 170 countries, BT Group provides communications solutions and services to people around the world. Its employees are located primarily across eight corporate offices throughout the United Kingdom, with additional operations in more than twenty-five locations. That keeps BT's corporate communications group busy. That's where Dennison works, creating the strategies, policies, and governance for the company's intranet. He saw that server—and the employee who saw the need for it—as a great opportunity to begin experimenting. The first social media tool BT put in place was "BTPedia," an enterprise-wide internal Wikipedia of sorts. (In fact, the software platform used is the same one that underpins Wikipedia.) Dennison wasn't the only one interested. Many other employees, including many college graduate hires, soon found BTPedia, and it began to gain momentum with employees sharing anything and everything that would help them do their jobs more effectively.

Because that seemed to go well, the company launched a pilot blogging platform using WordPress. WordPress took off, too. Increasing numbers of people found the blog site, initiated ideas, and contributed their thoughts. Up to that time, no corporate communication had been issued, and no promotional campaign had been launched. People just came. Next, BT decided to launch a very small social networking site. Suddenly, use went through the roof and blew up the little server under the desk! So Dennison had to close the social networking site and take the next step.

He quickly went to the IT group to request resources and infrastructure. But because social media was not yet a part of the company's IT road map, a slew of conversations ensued. In the end, IT saw that the platforms needed were free and easy to set up. So, the department helped Dennison support the social media craze at BT Group.

Nearly three years later, utilizing social media tools is a way of life at BT Group. The company's social networking site is properly supported and no longer "burns up" the server. BTPedia remains the most popular tool for employees to cocreate useful information. For example, a common practice that has emerged is the creation of "index pages." Employees create Web pages to catalogue useful links on a particular topic, pulling the information that is currently scattered throughout the intranet into one entry point. Incidentally, the most popular index page is titled "Recognition" and lists the five primary places where employees can give kudos to their colleagues for valuable contributions. Engagement is certainly alive and well.

The blogging platform continues to gain momentum. Podcast Central is the tool with which employees load and download user-generated audio files—important meetings or self-made training modules, for example—that they want to share with teammates. A discussion forum graces the front page of the online *Corporate Newsdesk*, a professional news e-zine managed by freelance journalists.

And one of the most valuable tools that BT Group employees gravitate to is the project wiki called Confluence. Project teams use Confluence as a centralized work space to house all their thoughts, documents, and resources. They can secure the access for members only, or open it up to greater input. With more than eight hundred thousand Web pages, this popular tool has proven its usefulness.

Dennison recognizes the maturity of the company's intranet and its employee workforce. "Our intranet is quite robust. It helps employees do most everything. But, prior to incorporating social media tools, the intranet didn't really support collaboration and relationship building. And that's what we really needed. These tools represent the next logical step for us."

Dennison is not trying to prove the return on investment for specific social media technology. In fact, he believes that such a measure is nearly impossible: "It's like opening the bonnet of a car, ripping the pieces out, and asking about the return due to one component. Each component contributes to the whole, so you have to measure the performance of the engine, not specific components within it. We don't have social media strategies; we have business strategies, and we look to see how social media can help us achieve them." Dennison knows instinctively that social media has enabled the organization to boost performance. For example, one of BT's key strategies is Right First Time, an effort to avoid re-work and save human and financial resources. The company's project wikis, blogs, and forums keep innovation high and expense low, ensuring that employees are more often able to be right the first time.

More important, Dennison is confident that the long-term benefits of BT's social media use will pay off for the company. "We really don't get the most from our employees because we limit the scope of their engagement. But social media invites them to participate beyond their immediate function. At the very basic level, the more people invest in their own company, in terms of developing networks and engaging in the wider organization, the more they invest in their own personal brand. Then, the more loyal they are and the less likely they are to leave because they've invested more."

Dennison notes that concerns initially existed about renegade employees who might act disrespectfully or inappropriately, but says the company has seen neither. He emphasizes that once an organization makes good use of social media, it makes everything it does transparent. Leaders must be willing to listen to other points of view, consider them as valuable information, and use this input to make better business decisions. In the end, employees simply want to know they've been heard. In BT's case, two specific uses of social media made a huge impact on its culture of trust. Several years ago, the previous CEO fostered communication in an unprecedented way by holding ninety-minute online chat sessions every six weeks. He responded in real time, uncensored and unedited, to employee questions and comments. Employees knew they were communicating directly and candidly with the CEO himself. He did this for seven years. Dennison still relates this example with excitement: "That one act blew the organization's culture wide open! In one step he connected the top of the organization to the bottom and gave people permission to participate more widely than before."

In a second similar example, current CEO Ian Livingston sent a powerful message to employees. At the time, he was the CEO of the retail division. He saw a discussion under way on the popular *Corporate Newsdesk* online and felt compelled to provide his point of view. But he did so in a way that employees read his comments as just another individual contribution, not as coming from the CEO. Once again, BT's culture of participation and engagement was strengthened from the bottom up and from the top down.

BT's journey has been a valuable experience, and the learning continues. Dennison's experiences have resulted in useful recommendations for all of us. One of these recommendations is to recognize that a "bottom-up" culture needs

TRAILBLAZER

top-down support to be successful. In addition, people learn by actually doing work, so it pays to let users experiment and "play" as early as possible—succeed or fail quickly ... and cheaply! Dennison also recommends engaging the organization's "watchdog" departments early (legal department, security, human resources) and emphasizes that embracing social media is an evolution, not a revolution. Lastly, Dennison counsels us to "start anywhere." "Start immediately ...and proceed until apprehended! Bottom line? Just start. Start small, build slowly, and follow the energy of trailblazers through the network."

In this chapter, we've shared how social media can strengthen five key organizational elements: attracting and retaining the best employees, innovation and knowledge creation, operational efficiency, talent development, and employee engagement. Through the connection, communication, and collaboration afforded by social media, employees or organizational members can do more together, faster, and in new ways.

Fueled by the power of social media, these five organizational elements become increasingly significant factors that can propel organizational performance. Cisco and BT are two examples of organizations that have recognized this opportunity and created a way for social media to assist in achieving their goals. In the next chapter, we'll discuss many more examples of social media at work in organizations.

Join the Conversation

Connect with others who, like you, are exploring, experimenting, and pioneering the use of social media to propel organizational performance. Go to www.socialmediaatwork-connection.com to ask your questions, learn what others are doing, and add your insights to the conversation. This chapter raises the following questions for you and your fellow community members:

- Where have you seen social media playing out in your organization or others?
- Where do you see the opportunities for social media in your organization?
- How have you seen social media used in other organizational areas to propel organizational performance?

5

EXAMPLES FROM TRAILBLAZERS

As a high school senior, Demetra Kassis was exploring where to apply for her university studies. She knew she wanted to attend an urban school on the Pacific Coast of North America, but which one? Demetra knew that she could research universities on the Internet. What she didn't know was that some universities used social networking sites and tools like Facebook and microblogging to capture her attention.

Something about the tweet that she received from the University of San Francisco (USF) caught her attention. It provided a link to the school's Web site. Founded in 1855, USF is the second-oldest institution of higher learning in the state of California, and the oldest in the city of San Francisco. A private Catholic university, it has a student body of nearly nine thousand, hosts students from seventy-five countries, and is ranked among the top fifteen most diverse universities. As Demetra explored the university's Web site, she came across its mission statement. Among USF's core values, the ones focused on diversity, social responsibility, service learning, and excellence in teaching and scholarly endeavors particularly appealed to Demetra. The university's use of social media attracted her attention and quickly captivated her interest. The incorporation of social media into the university enables USF to attract students who seek the best instructional strategies for their studies.

TRAILBLAZER

An increasing number of organizations are exploring how social media can help them become and remain competitive among their peers. Our increasingly complex environment, both at work and in our personal lives, demands that we employ tools to help us stay agile and adaptable. As we discussed in the previous chapter, the emerging phenomenon of social media positively influences the achievement of both short- and long-term goals. Increasing the knowledge, capability, and efficiency of employees today will help achieve the short-term goals of an organization's strategy. Social capital—the advantageous connections between individuals—and the continuous attention to talent development, retention, and engagement enable organizations to create a committed group of employees who can sustain that organization's success over the long run. Along with knowledge, both human and social capital can serve as intangible sources of an organization's sustainability.

Most of the current attention around social media is focused on how companies are using it to get closer to customers to increase brand awareness, generate business, and create customer loyalty. Engaging the customer through such media as blogging or twittering improves the company's visibility exponentially. We've discovered that many of the same companies that are using social media to create deeper connections *outside* their organizations, with customers, are also exploring how social media can help them *inside* the organization. But internal social connectivity presents some interesting dynamics. It challenges the traditional top-down formal communications and the informal watercooler rumor mill. It involves making changes to the existing collaboration processes, and accentuates the differences in the work style preferences of our four generations in the workforce. But despite these challenges and others, companies are finding it more risky to ignore the potential of social media inside their organizations. The brave ones jump in, experiment, learn, and improve in rapid cycles. Many organizations are blazing a trail for others to follow.

Our research for this book included pouring over academic research, trade books, current articles, and, as you might imagine, a plethora of blogs, wikis, microblogs, and social networking site chatter. However, it was our conversations with others through interviews and informal exchanges that led to the rich understanding of the potential of social media for organizations. The excitement and momentum found in these forward-thinking organizations is incredible. We call these companies the social media trailblazers.

Our social media trailblazers believe that this technology will strengthen the five elements we discussed in Chapter Four—(1) attracting and retaining the best employees, (2) innovation, (3) operational efficiency, (4) talent development, and (5) employee engagement—transforming them into factors that help drive short-term achievements as well as sustained competitiveness. We have sprinkled many examples throughout this book, but in this chapter we dive deeper into how social media is strengthening the aforementioned elements of success. In the following pages, we also share some of the best case studies of the companies we researched that are at the forefront of using social media. Although we've categorized the examples in terms of the five areas previously, we emphasize that they are usually inextricably intertwined. The elements are interdependent, and consequently an organization's use of social media can involve and have an impact on several of them at once. Nevertheless, we demarcate these factors here in hopes that we will enable you to see the impact social media can have in many areas of your organization.

Attracting and Retaining the Best Talent with Social Media

We all know that attracting talent is essential to an organization's viability. Whatever the economic climate, developing capable and agile talent enables smart organizations to thrive. Even as the demand for talent increases, the supply of this talent in many parts of the world will be decreasing. In addition, as competition becomes increasingly global, people are willing to change jobs often, given the right circumstances. Savvy organizations are finding social media a powerful tool in vying for the right candidates. Let's explore a few organizations that are using social media to their advantage in this war for talent.

Salesforce.com

As it battles for the best and brightest college graduates, salesforce.com knows it must be where those students hang out, so the company has joined social networking sites Facebook and LinkedIn.[1] The technologies also serve as a way for the company to keep in touch with new hires during the span of time between a fall recruiting cycle and their first day of work after graduation. Salesforce.com noticed early on that its newer employees, students, interns, and alumni have ultimate control in inviting people into the salesforce.com network using social media tools like Facebook. This is a more sincere, genuine recruitment strategy, and is a quasi-self-governing process, as contrasted with one directed by an official recruiting team.[2] Salesforce.com also integrates microblogging (Twitter) with its customer relationship management software. The company wants its best candidates to recognize the organization as leading edge, and the use of social media is evidence of this desire. All new hires experience it from the start of the recruiting cycle.

Salesforce.com is only one of many organizations that are actively working to attract and retain new Generation Y employees by using social media. Recruiters know that this target population expects, and in fact demands, the availability and usage of social computing tools. Many high-tech companies, such as Google, Microsoft, and Oracle, are also using social media technologies to attract recent college graduates.

The CIA

If you're beginning to think that using social media tools for recruiting is the exclusive domain of Silicon Valley high-tech companies, think again. Whereas being a spy may involve foreign languages, exotic travel, assumed identities, and secret codes, the process of *becoming* a spy is "out of the closet." These days, if you're interested in this type of work, all you need to do is pay attention to the advertising in various types of media. The Central Intelligence Agency (CIA) also uses social networking sites, such as Facebook; microblogging (Twitter); and even advertising on YouTube for the National Clandestine Activities division. Make no mistake, the CIA is not lacking candidates. This is an organization that truly searches for the best and the brightest young talent. But by using social media technologies, it is possibly more likely to attract the kind of tech-savvy candidates it seeks.

Oracle's OWL Community

Earlier we learned how Dow is tapping into the network of alumni and female employees. Another example of the use of social media to harness the power of diversity can be seen at work at Oracle. Oracle's Women's Leadership group (known as OWL) has become a thriving leadership development program. The purpose of OWL is to foster an environment to grow and retain future female top talent, enhance their skills, and empower Oracle women to step up to their greatest leadership potential. OWL began as a grassroots effort that was originally sponsored and funded by an Oracle executive VP. Enabled by social computing technologies, OWL has grown broadly across Oracle and expanded into a corporate-wide global program. Joyce Westerdahl, Oracle's senior VP of human resources and a member of OWL's steering committee, shared these thoughts about the value of OWL: "Our success and ability to remain competitive in the global marketplace depends on the ability of all of our employees to be successful at Oracle. OWL's unique structure and network provides opportunities for our next generation of female executives to further their professional development, creating a two-way formula for achieving success."

More specifically, Oracle employees have been developing and using leading-edge social software tools. As a community, OWL members have a portal, which includes a forum for blogging. Members can search for a wide range of resources, including announcements, suggestions for readings, links to industry resources, and links to professional career coaches. The portal also chats and virtual panel discussion forums. Clearly, social media technologies have enabled fast growth for a key talent pool. OWL's global and local communities support, educate, and empower the current and future generations of women leaders at Oracle.

The Roman Catholic Church

Whereas traditional organizations may focus on embracing diversity, other types of organizations are also jumping into the social media fray to harness the "talent potential" of their constituents. One such group includes organized religion. Since his election, Pope Benedict XVI has made determined efforts to keep Roman Catholicism in line with technological developments. While President Obama was being inaugurated, the Vatican launched its own channel on YouTube to keep Catholic worshippers current with the pope's activities and to celebrate "the capacity of the new technologies to foster and support good and healthy relationships and various forms of solidarity."[3] The pope's particular aim is to encourage young Catholics across the globe "to bring the witness of their faith to the digital world." This effort is aimed at the affinity group of Catholics; to date, it is not aimed at evangelizing potential converts to the religion. The use of social media works to connect a vastly diverse population whose common denominator is the members' religion.

Social Media and Innovation

Social networking advances a whole new frontier of organizational dialogue, setting the stage for continuous knowledge creation and organizational agility. It brings people together as a community. Just what is the role of community in today's organizations? In *Cultivating Communities of Practice*, Wenger, McDermott, and Snyder argue that communities of practice are vital to success in a global knowledge economy.[4] They caution that organizations are competing for market share, but also for much more: they are also competing for key talent—those people who can make a pivotal difference in the ability to become market leaders and to attract venture capital.

Of course, all this theoretical grounding is notable, but the proof is in the pudding. Read any newspaper—traditional or on the Internet—and your head may spin from the various stories about how technologies are being used to solicit customer feedback and track trends to competitive advantage. But just how are organizations using social media *internally* in ways that are useful and innovative?

Geek Squad

Geek Squad was founded in 1994 and is now a wholly owned subsidiary of Best Buy. The heart of Geek Squad's mission is to provide commercial technical support for home PC users. Of course, the company does it with a unique brand, replete with black shoes, white socks, black pants, white shirts, and clip-on ties. Geek Squad employees have also learned to leverage social media technologies for knowledge creation and innovation: "Geek Squad employees use wikis, video games, and all kinds of unorthodox collaboration technologies to brainstorm new ideas, manage projects, swap service tips [and] even contribute to product innovation and marketing."[5]

Geek Squad employees used wikis to design and implement an entirely new product line, consisting of flash drives with retractable USB connectors, for parent company Best Buy, garnering prestigious technical design awards along the way. Support agents have even learned to collaborate while playing online multiplayer video games with each other. One key lesson that Geek Squad has gained from its experience in innovating via social media is that to inspire organizational knowledge creation and innovation, technology-enabled collaboration must emerge organically from the employees themselves, rather than as the product of top-down mandates.

Philips

Beyond using wikis as a collaborative tool for innovation, some companies are also experimenting with the use of Second Life as a tool for innovation. As mentioned earlier, Second Life (SL) is a free online virtual world—with people, entertainment, education, businesses, and so on—that is created by its imaginative residents. In SL, participants can make land purchases, including private islands that can be used for any number of purposes, such as business, education through virtual campuses, political use in campaigns, recreation, to conduct trade, and so on. Some groups purchase private islands and share the expenses among members; this way they know that all their neighbors are members of their own unique group.

Philips, a diversified health and well-being global company, prides itself on its timely innovations and is now experimenting with SL for product development in the area of lighting. It is hosting teams of four to six people and working with internal facilitators on small private islands to interact with product concepts and to participate in roundtable discussions across the globe. Philips designers are using SL to challenge users to think differently and to explore new scenarios.[6]

Oracle

At enterprise software giant, Oracle, engineers use wikis extensively in their development work as they collaborate across the globe in the 24/7 working environment. Although product developers use all types of traditional methods to create products, wikis enable the brightest minds to collaborate and cogenerate product ideas that are not only innovative but also capable of being swiftly adopted and produced. Oracle's engineers use blogs and wikis as primary tools for reporting on work progress and coordinating work with one another. People request and provide backups when needed, and the data are highly accessible, enabling managers to allocate and redistribute resources to critical projects.

In addition to its wikis and blogs, the company has its own microblogging capability, Oratweet. As mentioned in Chapter Three, Oracle latched on to Oratweet as a way for engineers to bridge communication gaps within their global teams. Microblogging is an effective way to alert team members of successes, challenges, best practices, and tidbits of useful information. It's not disruptive, nor is it obtrusive like traditional e-mail; people can grab what they want, when they want it.

Social Media and Operational Efficiency

As introduced earlier, operational efficiency occurs when organizations pull together the right mix of talent, processes, and technologies to enhance the productivity and value of their operations, while also driving down the cost of routine transactions. Having achieved such efficiency, organizations can shift resources to initiatives with higher impact. The end result is that resources previously needed to manage operational tasks can be redirected to new, high-value initiatives that bring additional capabilities or results to the organization.

The Obama Campaign

A notable example of enhanced operational efficiency through the use of social media is Barack Obama's 2008 U.S. presidential campaign. A significant strength of this campaign was its creative use of Internet tools, both on public sites and within the campaign's organization. It also used a collaboration platform to scale its grassroots efforts in many states, organizing and collaborating with thousands of voting precincts. The Obama campaigners were looking for a competitive advantage over other presidential hopefuls and were able to extend their reach beyond traditional methods through the creative use of such social media as MySpace, Facebook, YouTube, and Twitter.

One ardent Obama supporter was Chris Hughes, a cofounder of Facebook. He parlayed his passion to elect Obama into an innovative political campaign that focused in large part on online discussions hosted by the Web site MyObama.com. According to *Fast Company*, Hughes helped develop the "most robust set of Web-based social-networking tools ever used in a political campaign, enabling energized citizens to turn themselves into activists, long before a single human field staffer arrived to show them how."[7] Part of the campaign's strength rested in how volunteers leveraged wikis, blogs, microblogs, and other Web 2.0 tools to scale grassroots efforts.

Let's explore how the wiki was used in the Obama campaign. According to an article by Sarah Lai Stirland of *Wired*, the Obama campaign team used Central Desktop's wiki tools to quickly organize and publish meeting locations, materials, contact points, and instructions for campaign staff and organizers.[8] The wiki-based tool allowed for rapid content development in the few weeks leading up to select state campaigns (for example, Texas, California, Ohio) and was maintained and updated by volunteers. The campaigners also used an online training tool for precinct captains that enabled better management and tracking of volunteer canvassers. When precinct captains returned from their "block walks," they entered the results of their efforts into the database, logging which households had Obama boosters, who was caucusing, and who was willing to volunteer. They were able to capture the names and contact information of people who were willing to assist in precinct campaigning and to keep each other updated.

David Carr of the *New York Times* reported that the Obama campaign bolted several social networking applications together, which "created an unforeseen force to raise money, organize locally, fight smear campaigns and get out the vote that helped them topple Hilary Clinton and later the Republican Presidential candidate, John McCain.[9] With a database of millions of supporters' names, President Obama entered the White House poised to engage instantly with his constituency. Immediately after his election, he e-mailed his supporters, writing "We have a lot of work to do to get our country back on track, and I'll be in touch soon about what comes next." Obama's team fulfilled that promise by establishing a Web site for the transition, and then in the White House through http://www.whitehouse.gov.

In short, social media tools enabled Obama campaigners to organize themselves differently and to keep interactions timely, creating a campaign that was more efficient and effective. The campaign was extremely successful at extending its reach by navigating the complexity of the American political landscape through innovative and creative use of social media. Ultimately, such technologies helped solidify the 2008 victory and changed the face of politics in the United States. But Obama wasn't the only innovative politician; other candidates were some of the early adopters of social media as well: Mitt Romney used salesforce.com to track campaign expenses, and Howard Dean used blogging and a meeting organizing tool (www.meetup.com) to raise more money than other Democratic candidates prior to the 2004 Iowa caucuses.

IBM

The discipline of "knowledge management" was popularized in corporate America during the 1990s. Employees stored information and documents for others to use with the promise of saving time and not "reinventing the wheel." However, many companies did not receive the benefits they had anticipated. IBM's previous efforts in knowledge management stalled for the same reason such efforts failed in most organizations: the process was too structured for employees, and they continued to retain critical tacit knowledge in their minds. In 2006, IBM began using its own social networking tool, Community Tools, to enable employees to help each other solve their problems in record time. Employees type a question and post it to the online community, and many people instantly offer solutions. In fact, if more than ten people respond to the question, the tool creates an instant community chat site to enable their conversation. For IBM this is not only a powerful collaboration and innovation tool, but also a key means of speeding up time for problem solving and decision making.[10]

The LDS Church

The Church of Jesus Christ of Latter-day Saints (LDS Church) highlights a unique way in which social media can advance efficiency in organizations with nontraditional operational structures. One of the fastest-growing Christian denominations, the LDS Church is "run" by a lay (unpaid volunteer) ministry consisting of its almost fourteen million members. Many members have started leveraging social media to communicate more efficiently at regional and local levels. For example, a regional "mid-singles" group (between the ages of twenty-seven and forty-five) in the San Francisco Bay Area has established blogs on MySpace to notify members of its activities. Once limited to making phone calls and distributing flyers to local congregations, this group is now using social media–enabled "viral marketing" to publicize events.

A recent summer extravaganza in California attracted over a thousand single members from more than ten U.S. states and as far as Europe and Japan.

Likewise, the church's semiannual conference in Salt Lake City is now broadcast to members across the globe using real-time streaming media and podcasting. The conference recently became the top discussion item on Twitter for a weekend as members tweeted each other about various conference topics. LDS leaders are currently discussing additional ways to leverage social media in building a sense of community, fellowship, and engagement. Church headquarters in Salt Lake City has even launched an online Tech Forum to solicit input from members and nonmembers about employing technology more efficiently in the church's operations. According to LDS church leaders, social media helps accelerate the church's mission "with a thousandfold greater speed and ease" than was possible in biblical times.[11]

Hewlett-Packard

Hewlett-Packard Company (HP) has an extremely large workforce distributed across the world, and it is common for collaboration to span many departments and geographic regions. Consequently, the company has begun to use social media in its efforts to improve effectiveness. One tool they've created to speed collaboration is an online community called *WaterCooler*. Developed in 2007, WaterCooler mimics the familiar gathering place in corporate offices but allows much greater reach for employees' thoughts. Any content posted on WaterCooler is "public" to all HP employees and contractors, and posting authors are identified by name.

Scientists at HP Labs, the company's internal think tank, are studying the use and impact of WaterCooler on company performance.[12] So far, their findings have indicated that people use WaterCooler as an effective method for learning what other people in the company are doing. Overall, a majority of survey respondents have noted that WaterCooler has changed their perceptions of collaboration at HP.

Some individuals have reported that WaterCooler makes the company feel "a little smaller and more human."[13] Another user commented that social media personalizes the organization, and makes it "real." Others within the company have noticed that social media creates collegiality in a time of economic uncertainty. Global emergencies create a lot of hum at the WaterCooler. In one incident a number of HP employees let colleagues across the world know they were safe after a fire closed an HP facility in Southern California.

WaterCooler's value in cultivating beneficial employee relationships and operational efficiency is compelling. Its tagging feature is particularly useful. Employees tag such topics as hobbies, interests, products, projects, skills, and teams. But most notably, research results have shown that online people-tagging through this tool has enabled faster formation of virtual teams, quicker orientation to the organization for newcomers, and a greater sense of engagement. WaterCooler has also helped to accelerate innovation by enabling employees to find the right internal expertise and knowledge faster than they could do so previously.[14] In addition, with all the information that bombards employees every day, WaterCooler provides a way for team members to signal what's important and where they should place their attention. The tool helps project teams in particular achieve their goals more effectively. They come to WaterCooler for brainstorming, sharing project milestones, and simple logistical updates.

To be sure, there are several barriers that hinder the adoption of tools like WaterCooler. HP has mentioned time constraints, unequal participation, and the clamor for attention by competing electronic voices. Through their WaterCooler experience, HP has learned several important lessons about the adoption of social media. They note the need for management sponsorship, adequate IT support, and open data access. Despite these challenges, findings have indicated that WaterCooler offers tremendous business value. The use of social media has increased employees' sense of connection to the company's initiatives and to each other. We all know that business gets done over lunch or at the company watercooler. HP's WaterCooler accelerates business operations in ways many employees would never have imagined a decade ago.

Social Media and Talent Development

Employee training and development teams are also finding innovative uses of social media to share knowledge, develop skills, and manage talent. The ability to easily and quickly share knowledge, learning, and wisdom helps create a learning culture. Social media enables continuous on-the-job learning, and allows employees to see how to apply new skills in real time and in real work situations.

Detroit's Henry Ford Hospital

Detroit's Henry Ford Hospital broke new ground in 2009 with "just-in-time" and "real-time" learning for medical school students.[15] Not only did the hospital use online video feeds to give students a "play-by-play" view into surgery, but it also pioneered the use of microblogging for other interested parties. During surgery on a forty-seven-year-old patient with a brain tumor, a technician installed a computer in one corner of the operating room to give feeds on YouTube. (Of course, the patient consented to the YouTube video feeds and the microblogging prior to the surgery.)

At home, medical students could watch the YouTube feeds as the surgeons exposed the patient's brain. This enabled the students to get a close-up view of the procedure. The real power of the technology is that it gave medical students an "up close and personal" view into the surgeon's decision-making processes. Through the microblogging, the doctors were able to field and answer questions that had been tweeted from around the country.

The doctors answered these questions as they emerged from the actual surgery.

Dr. Kalkanis, one of the primary surgeons, indicated that using these types of technologies advances the frontier and educates as many people as possible. Kalkanis also noted that it is vital for educators to communicate with the tools that the current generation of students uses: "It's a generation skilled in instant, interactive, interpersonal communication and feedback, and I think that if medical education is going to be as relevant and effective as possible, it needs to keep pace with this new standard."[16]

Cisco

Cisco is exploring social media in many aspects of its business. As we saw in Chapter Four, the use of social media is playing an increasingly important role in its learning solutions development and delivery process. This networking company inherently understands the power of social computing and constantly searches for ways to use technology to improve its business. The case we shared in Chapter Four about the Cisco Development Organizations (CDO) course development and delivery shows how Cisco is forging ahead with new applications of social media for collaborative design, delivery, and improved learning solutions. As we noted, this one project alone saved Cisco 90 percent of the cost associated with traditional methods of training deployment, not to mention the cost savings from eliminating all travel expenses for twenty-five hundred employees. Greg Brower (CDO Curriculum Planning) and Linda Chen (program manager) for this effort drove the learning solution to meet Cisco's business strategies of innovation, cost savings, scale, and employee engagement.[17]

Coaches Training Institute

The Coaches Training Institute (CTI) is one of the premier organizations that trains and certifies professional business and life coaches around the world. The rigorous training that CTI brings to its students is a fully blended approach and demonstrates CTI's commitment to the power of relationships. CTI has been effectively using various forms of social media for several years. Through its Internet portal, it provides an extensive resource network for all its members (current students and alumni) to assemble in one central community. Through this electronic network, CTI members can continue to improve their coaching skills, participate in CTI-sponsored lectures and events, keep up-to-date on new developments in the coaching field, and continually interact with other CTI members, exchanging ideas and information.

Beyond this central hub, CTI offers many niche and geographic communities to its coaching constituents. Members come together to create learning, share resources, cultivate alliances, develop opportunities, and build community niches. Hundreds of coaches access CTI's portal every day to update their profiles, conduct polling, share announcements, identify useful resources, host public discussions, check a calendar, and search for members.

CTI's training and certification process consists of a notable design. The first phase of the program is a six month series of face-to-face workshops in the trainees' local area; the second phase of the program involves a much broader community of coaches from around the world. Coaches are placed into small groups of nine, and meet with each other once a week for instruction, practice, and discussion—but they never meet each other in person. All their correspondence, curriculum, materials, and resources are found on their community Web site. This hub of information is their lifeline. It includes social networking capabilities, search functions, video, podcasts, and a wide range of special interest groups for networking. Most important, participants in the certification program go there to blog each week. Blogging enables them to reflect on their coaching practice, ask common questions, give each other tips, and learn from each other's experiences. This worldwide program would not be as successful as it is without the use of social media tools.

Oracle's Global Organization and Talent Development Group

Oracle is aggressively utilizing social media technologies to enhance the learning and development investments it makes in its employees. Earlier in this chapter, we shared how Oracle is using wikis and forums for product development and how it is using forums and social networking community spaces to engage women leaders in new ways. As we saw in Chapter Three, Oracle is using social media in a variety of other ways as well. One of the most beneficial uses is in the area of talent development.

The Global Organization and Talent Development group is incorporating social media into most of its development solutions and consulting services. One example is the Global Leadership Academy, a talent development program that was aimed at high-potential senior leaders across the globe in the services engineering group. The one-year program maintained a strong focus on leading strategic business initiatives and collaborating across functional and geographic boundaries. Each of the three initiative teams included leaders from different functions and locations. To maintain the momentum of their progress and the richness of the learning within and between each team, the program included a wiki as a home base for their projects, a discussion forum to maintain their dialogue, and numerous live webinar sessions. The results of the program included three successful business improvements and a layer of leaders more ready to take on executive roles.

Social Media and Employee Engagement

Ongoing studies and research have identified the mutually reinforcing relationship between business performance and a culture of engagement. Culture correlates with retention and influences profitability by lowering the cost of human capital, including recruiting costs.[18] A culture of collaboration and contribution allows for greater use of social media experimentation and enables employees to be more engaged, have greater purpose, and feel that they make a difference. Each of the following examples represents ways that social networking and other social media tools can enhance positive organizational culture and engagement.

Best Buy

Recent research has demonstrated that job performance, team performance, and creativity are higher when employees are included in well-developed social networks.[19] Best Buy, for example, used its internal social networking community, Blue Shirt Nation, to reinforce it culture of mentoring. As Geek Squad discovered, for true engagement to occur, the company culture had to support collaboration. The CEO noted that it took years to cultivate the culture of pride, identity, and purpose.[20]

Oracle

An information technology pundit observed that social software exposes the extent to which "people inside organizations are looking for change, the depth of undiscovered creativity, and the value of collaboration." If social technology implementation is handled poorly, the workforce can be dis-incentivized.[21]

The employees at Oracle took this advice to heart, and the company is nurturing a connected culture with smart policies and robust feature enhancements, all the while listening to the groundswell of internal employee preferences. Because many employees have come to work at Oracle via an acquisition, team members have become more geographically dispersed. Consequently, the organization was searching for a tool to help employees feel a part of one culture, connect with those who can help them, and contribute to a wider range of projects. Enter Oracle Connect. Created by a small team of passionate engineers, Oracle Connect had no big communications splash, no corporate e-mail, no sponsored announcement. Instead, it simply appeared, and within a few short days, participation was increasing exponentially.

With Oracle Connect, employees create their own profile and can include information they want to share. Common information includes the nature of their current work, what they've done in the past, and any other relevant skills and experiences. Oracle Connect provides an indexing feature so that employees can type in keywords and return profiles containing those keywords. Because work at Oracle is collaborative in general, expanding their personal network helps employees by enabling them to share ideas with a wider audience. In a company where knowledge is prized, individuals want to be known as a source of knowledge and expertise, and those who need it want to find those people quickly. Oracle Connect helps employees expand their reach in an ever-changing environment. It also keeps everyone abreast of the latest tools that can help them contribute more effectively. Smart engineers find it both challenging and fun to ensure access to emerging technologies, such as Apple's iPhone and other new devices that the new generations at work demand. To them, this is engagement.

Indirectly, more junior engineers or those newer to Oracle are encouraged to join the fray. These newer employees are receiving a de facto type of mentoring through this process, and they come "up to speed" quickly. Through social media, they can fully participate in any effort, and their contributions are immediately valued and considered. Not only does this tool enable new employees to engage early on, but capturing this additional input has a direct impact on the bottom line by decreasing product development cycle time.

IBM

IBM is another large organization that has been aggressively launching various social media tools internally in the belief that these tools can cultivate a culture of engagement and contribution. Once new employees have been hired, organizations typically want to see their newly hired staff members come up to speed quickly. The term *on-boarding* typically refers to the activities used to help new employees integrate and become productive more quickly. IBM is one among many companies using social technologies to enhance the on-boarding process, which has moved far beyond the traditional classroom "new employee orientation" workshops. For example, the company uses Second Life for new employees—creating more efficient and effective process to ramp-up the learning curve and help them become productive faster.[22]

IBM continues to look for ways to keep employees engaged and productive throughout their careers. The Research Division is exploring how hot new technologies can work successfully and effectively in business. A few of IBM's tools include the following: Dogear (a community tagging system based on Delicious), Blue Twit (microblogging), and Many Eyes, a Web portal that enables people to upload all types of data, visualize it, and launch discussions about it on blogs and social networks.

By far, IBM's most successful social media tool is Beehive—an internal, voluntary social networking application. One very popular Beehive feature is the "top five" list. Employees make lists of the top five of anything they choose, such as the five projects they're most proud of, five technologies they can't live without, and so on. Beehive mixes personal and professional information, and each employee decides where the boundaries rest for himself or herself. The software also allows users to drag and drop information into their profiles. All this leads to self-branding; employees depict themselves as they choose. Searching is currently done via people's names and various tags. Although Beehive was initially a "bottom-up" tool, a key testament of its usefulness is that senior executives were early adopters.[23]

Dow

Most new college hires in any company are from the Millennial generation. As we noted earlier, this generation is interested in collaboration, connections, and contribution. But whatever they do, they want to do it very quickly. Because Millennials leverage social media in their everyday lives, organizations are finding that they must embed these tools into their work processes to keep from disengaging such valuable talent.

As we have also seen, the demand for talent continues to increase, while the supply in many parts of the world is decreasing. This environment, coupled with the new career life cycle and the willingness of Gen Y workers to change jobs, poses an increasing challenge for organizations in attracting, engaging, and retaining their most valuable human resources, no matter what their generation.

So, many organizations are asking themselves, How can we leverage social networking for greatest advantage among at least four distinct generations working in the workforce together? How will we foster an improved cultural climate and engagement when Millennials may demand this technology and others avoid it? Some organizations are capitalizing on the loyalty of former employees as well as alumni through the active support of social media connections.

Dow Chemical Company is a diversified enterprise that delivers a broad range of products and services to customers in over 160 countries, with some forty-five thousand employees that connect chemistry and innovation to help provide everything from fresh water, food, and pharmaceuticals to paints, packaging, and personal care products. As we saw in Chapter Two, there were four primary drivers for Dow's particular interest in social networking strategies: the anticipated loss of 40 percent of its workforce, the increasing demand for talent with the right knowledge, the need to retain its current talent, and the need to hire and retain more women in its workforce.

Dow's social networking site, My Dow Network, serves as a clear example of how organizations can use social technologies to link with valued populations. This site targets four different Dow groups: current employees, women, alumni, and retirees. When the social network was launched in 2007, its primary goal was to give access to organizational memory and to enable mentorship and cultural continuity for all employees. The network is an effective vehicle to engage current employees *and* tap into the energy and wisdom of former employees.

The My Dow Network design team identified several requirements for the site. These requirements included a "relationship search engine" to locate other current and former employees; a section with opportunities to reenter Dow on a full-time, part-time, or project basis; and a spotlight for retirees to show who has come back into the Dow workforce. Many retirees also expressed a desire to contribute to community success by sharing ideas and opportunities for volunteerism. Ultimately, the site has served as a hub for timely news about Dow and its employees.

Dow has metrics in place to track productivity, new business creation, employee engagement, and employee retention. Dow leaders believed that My Dow Network could help improve their business, and during the first year after launching the site, Dow achieved some of the significant goals that it had set. One key goal was to fill some of the needed external contractor positions with former retirees; in the initial twelve months, Dow retirees filled over 10 percent of the contractor roles. Further, Dow tracked more than forty-five hundred network members during the first three months of participation. Network users also generated over ten thousand position referrals for the company. In addition, Dow internal benchmarking against other multinational Fortune 500 companies led to the conclusion that My Dow Network ranked in the top 50 percent of similar programs in other organizations.

The creation of My Dow Network was a collaborative effort of several functions within Dow: workforce planning, diversity and inclusion, public affairs, human resources, and various business units. This team's keys to success were that they identified an external service provider; identified four social networking audiences—retirees, former employees, women who left to have children, and current employees; and gained the support and sponsorship of senior management.

Using social media to link and engage current employees, former employees, women, and retirees has brought many benefits to all involved: it has supported knowledge transfer and the mentoring of new employees, encouraged retirees to serve as "brand ambassadors," enabled stronger connections with key stakeholder groups, facilitated targeted communications, and offered the continued opportunity for these affinity groups to contribute in valuable ways, ultimately enhancing the reputation of the organization.[24]

Intel

Although new hires have a great deal to contribute, the benefit of their contribution is often delayed as they acclimate to their work environment. This situation is common in many industries; yet, Intel Corporation is capitalizing on the advent of social computing technologies to play a key role in addressing this demand from newer college recruits to become productive as soon as possible.

Intel's recruiters know that Gen Y workers expect and demand the availability of social computing tools. Therefore, they use these tools to attract recent college graduates. However, in 2009, Intel established an additional goal to improve the "time to integration" of new hires by 45 percent by the end of the year. The company realized that new recruits want their voices to be heard. Without this immediacy, that is, to have access to information, to get to know people, and to start contributing quickly, new hires disengage and leave, particularly in regions where competitors can woo them away with attractive incentives. Using internal metrics, Intel has determined that it is, in fact, achieving reduced time to integration. The availability of social networking, not only during recruitment but also during matriculation, is having an impact. New hires have indicated that they are matriculating quickly and ramping up well to perform their jobs productively.

Trailblazer—Nokia Embraces Social Media

One innovative company that demonstrates the use of social media to strengthen all five of the elements we've discussed is Nokia Corporation. Headquartered in Finland, Nokia is a large, global company with over 128,000 employees in 120 countries; it is the world's largest manufacturer of mobile telephones. Let's take a closer look at the way Nokia is using social media to create a culture of full employee engagement while producing innovative products and services.

In 2007, senior managers at Nokia declared that it would embrace the Internet wholeheartedly. For Jere Korhonen, a manufacturing engineer working at global headquarters just outside Helsinki, this was interesting news. Jere wondered about what impact this move would have on the core values at Nokia, and he wasn't the only employee to question what this meant. Nokia employees were concerned about how the company would need to change to achieve this objective.

One of the most appealing aspects of Nokia is its culture. It was Nokia's culture of openness, respect for individuals, and teamwork that attracted Jere and many others to the company. Despite its large size, Nokia had a culture that emphasized speed, flexibility, and decision making in a rather flat, egalitarian way. Until May 2007, the core values espoused by Nokia and noted in the corporate manifesto, the Nokia Way, were customer satisfaction, respect, achievement, and renewal. What would Nokia need to change in the quest to become a world-class Internet-savvy company?

TRAILBLAZER

TRAILBLAZER

Senior leaders challenged the organization development and internal communications teams to come up with an approach that would model the Internet and Web 2.0. They developed a unique "high-touch, high-tech" approach that would ultimately connect all employees around the globe with this initiative and lead to a noteworthy set of outcomes that are relevant today.

Matthew Hanwell, senior manager of New Web Experiences in Nokia's organizational development and change team, was deeply involved in the processes and communication vehicles that Nokia created for incorporating these new values.[25] As Hanwell noted, various new hubs were created to ensure that relevant information was accessible to all employees. The hubs were also designed to be engaging to Nokia employees. Consequently, Nokia invested in the creation of several tools that together create a new way of communicating, connecting, and collaborating.

Employees embraced the launch of this new internal communication tool, called the NewsHub, where employees rate, vote, and comment on story content. Another employee communication hub that was launched is Blog Hub, created to consolidate numerous disparate blogs across the company. It offers an easily accessible place for employees to share their thoughts and opinions. Anyone can see what's happening, what people are sharing, what people are voting on, and article ratings. This gives employees like Jere a way to participate in a global Nokia discussion. A Manager Blog also allows leaders to share thoughts and opinions, using the same features as the other blogs. In addition, Nokia created a highly popular Video Hub, capitalizing on the YouTube phenomenon. With Video Hub, every employee is able to upload videos, vote on them, rate them, comment on them, and so on.

The organization is certainly leveraging social media in multiple innovative ways for employee communications and engagement. As might be anticipated, employees use their personal Nokia devices with video cameras to share newsworthy stories. In fact, the change management team seized on the idea of hosting a competition to link Nokia's corporate values with this natural part of the company's culture.[26] Here's what happened.

Recognizing the need for new skills in social media, the company invested in the development of two hundred employees called Nokia Reporters, who had the mission of reporting on "values in action." The Nokia Reporters learned how to make higher-quality stories in a video format: what makes a good story; how to script the story, record it, edit it, and post it. Then a series of large-scale change workshops were held in specific global locations to review, refine, and share the corporate values. These workshops engaged more than twenty-five hundred employees both face-to-face and virtually. The Nokia Reporters captured the stories and published the values for all to see.

A competition commenced after the values were published. Individuals across the company were asked to submit their personal examples of the values in action using their own phones as well as other social media tools, such as YouTube. Employees responded with artistic flare! Their submissions were posted on the Video Hub, and everyone in the company voted for the submissions that best embodied Nokia's values in action. Winners rose to the top of the Web site and into Nokia history.

Through the use of social media technologies—their own technologies!—Nokia was able to pull together stories of the people behind Nokia's products and services, design, future technologies, environment, and business goals. Through the creative and innovative use of social media, Nokia engaged its entire workforce and renewed its values: Engaging You, Achieving Together, Passion for Innovation, and Very Human. In turn, these core values support and advance Nokia's business strategy.

This single example illustrates many of the forces that propel organizational performance. Openness, sharing, and trusting are fundamental parts of the Nokia DNA. Employees were asked to contribute creatively, and they did in great numbers! Nokia developed the new skills it would need as an Internet company by using social media strategically. It fostered employee innovation and engaged its entire workforce in a meaningful and enjoyable way, gaining shared commitment to the company's corporate values. The company also saved great expense by using social media tools to create the desired virtual dialogue and exchange. It demonstrated its own corporate values of engagement and innovation with a creative and fun way of empowering employees. No doubt, this experience will pay long-term dividends in the retention of Nokia's talent. Moreover, as the story is shared and echoed over time, the next generation of Nokia employees will become increasingly eager to build their careers in the company as well.

Start with What Matters Most

Throughout this chapter, we have focused on the forces that improve performance today and sustain it into the future. For example, rapid innovation and knowledge creation naturally lead to shorter cycle times and faster speed-to-market. But they also keep your top talent interested and inspired. Although profitability definitely plays a critical role in the sustainability of an enterprise, macro- and microeconomic cycles invariably fluctuate between periods of growth and periods of stagnation or decline. We are in no way arguing that the use of social media *always* increases a company's profitability, although in many cases it does.

Organizations are challenged to identify the best ways to use social media to their benefit. In this chapter, we've shared how several of the social media trailblazers are incorporating these tools into their everyday business operations. We hope that this has sparked new ideas for how you can benefit from the use of these tools in your organization. Always start with the foundation of your business—its purpose, goals, and key strategies. As we saw with Nokia, the company knew the core of its business values and the importance of engaging its creative workforce. USF also knows its core purpose in attracting the brightest students who will thrive on its campus. These very different organizations and the many others in this chapter all found ways for social media to improve their current organizational performance.

Even if you want to cultivate the use of social media in your organization, it is still new territory. Implementing these strategies is one thing, but gaining true adoption by your organization is another. In the next chapter, we'll share a useful "playbook"—recommendations from the social media trailblazers for getting social media to work in your organization.

Join the Conversation

Connect with others who, like you, are exploring, experimenting, and pioneering the use of social media to propel organizational performance. Go to www.socialmediaatwork-connection.com to ask your questions, learn what others are doing, and add your insights to the conversation. This chapter raises the following questions for you and your fellow community members:

- Which of these trailblazers has goals similar to those of your organization?
- How can you combine ideas from the trailblazers to find valuable starting points for social media in your organization?
- How can you augment what you are already doing by adding social media to one of the five organizational forces for performance?

6

PUTTING SOCIAL MEDIA TO WORK

Emergent Solutions, Inc., is a global leadership and organization development consulting firm headquartered in Palo Alto, California. With an extended team of more than sixty-five trusted and skilled consultants across the globe, Emergent Solutions considers collaboration one of its hallmarks. The company actually refers to its network of consultants as "the Guild," connoting the supportive interaction that has been essential to its success.

Social media has played a large role in Emergent Solutions' productivity, improving its collaboration and streamlining its operations. Says Chris Cavanaugh-Simmons, managing director, "Precisely a year ago, circumstances conspired to get me to look at social networks. An acquaintance told me that I should look into social networking and wikis, and recommended that I read up on it. The first thing that struck me was how Emergent Solutions' goals and values meshed perfectly with the principles of a wiki: being open, peering, sharing, and acting globally. So I got incredibly excited about the possibilities."

Chris realized that as Emergent Solutions grew, it had increased client projects globally, but was not adequately leveraging the collective intelligence of its skilled consultant community. It subsequently missed opportunities for synergy, innovation, and agile responses to clients. Emergent Solutions also had to focus on operational processes and basic workflow. Cavanaugh-Simmons remembers how frustrating this was: "We'd been buried in the transactional processes needed to run our business, and our high-level strategies and long-range dreams were temporarily on hold."

Enter social media. Emergent Solutions' initial primary tool of choice was a wiki because of its intrinsic value as a tool for community collaboration. The company looked at several solutions, and finally selected SocialText as its partner.

To date, Emergent Solutions has developed several wiki workspaces:

- The Community Space for sharing current topics, events, discussions, resources, best practices, and lessons for improving internal effectiveness or customer solutions.

- A "design lab" for the full-time staff to post projects for tracking, visibility, accountability, and transparency

- A "wiki hub" accessed via Emergent Solutions' Web site, where clients can go without a password to learn and share insights regarding strategy, leadership, and organizational challenges. Emergent Solutions consultants often post current research and lessons gleaned from their ongoing work experiences.

- A Strategy as Narrative wiki for the community of consultants, external thought leaders, and customers who have assisted in the creation of this new premier offering.

- Private client spaces set up to capture insights, questions, and ideas in ongoing executive coaching relationships or consulting engagements.

The benefits have been clear. Playing on the term "Web 2.0," Emergent Solutions now uses the term Consulting 2.0 in explaining to clients how its collaborative approach delivers better results quicker. According to Cavanaugh-Simmons, "We call social media a utility. It has become a critical component of our operation—it's just as important to us as the light and the heat." Emergent Solutions has seen clear improvement in the quality of its service for its clients as well as in operational efficiencies. Once, for example, a customer sent a difficult request to Cavanaugh-Simmons, and she immediately blasted the request to the Guild. The collective responses were captured on the wiki, and Chris was able to review their input, transfer it to a document, and deliver it to the customer overnight. She "wowed" the client with her speed and depth of insight. "We really walk the talk in using Web 2.0 to enable our Consulting 2.0 strategies of partnering, transparency, and agility," says Chris. "This is a great way to illustrate to our client how our global capabilities and collaborative power add value."

In fact, the use of social media has improved Emergent Solutions' internal processes so much that the company was able to avoid hiring a full-time employee. Of course implementing social media wasn't easy. Many of Emergent Solutions' highly experienced consultants were not as tech savvy as they wanted to be, and some of Emergent Solutions' previous technology implementation efforts had fizzled. However, Emergent Solutions' partner, Social-Text, was responsive in smoothing out technical glitches and improving features.

Cavanaugh-Simmons viewed Emergent Solutions' implementation of social media as successful in part because the company viewed the process just as it would any complex organizational change for its own customers. Here are some of the lessons learned:

- Share the vision and begin the conversation. First get the partners aligned, then key staff, then the larger community, so that everyone can see where you're headed, why, and how it will benefit the organization and the customer.

- Be absolutely dogged in requiring people to use the new tools. Provide ample training for team members. Follow up and hold them accountable to the new processes. And, after a reasonable period, disable the old infrastructure, leaving no choice but to adapt to the new way of working.

- Repeat your communications more times that you ever thought necessary. For Emergent Solutions, "It's on the wiki" became a mantra until team members finally learned to go there for all answers.

- Make it fun to explore and adopt Web 2.0. For example, in one meeting, guild members counted the number of times the founding partners said the word *wiki*.

- Create an effective architecture and common templates that suit the needs of the business processes and that speed cocreation.

- Be patient and willing to have a messy process for a while. Don't get too attached to anything as a static element—learn to blow things up and rearrange processes to improve their usefulness.

- Identify a "gardener." The person with this critical role monitors and "cleans up" the initial wiki content so that as team members access the tool, they can easily find what they need, and they can easily contribute content. The gardener prunes overgrown content, transplants data to the best location, and ensures that any online space is inviting. Emergent Solutions felt that this seemingly minor item was an absolutely vital success factor.

- Be tenacious with leadership commitment. Emergent Solutions' founding partners never wavered in their certainty of the value of their wiki utility, and this overt passion was evident to their community. Dave Simpson, a consultant in the Guild, led one of the first internal projects. He noted, "Chris was so intentional about this being a community effort. There was no double-talk and no fear of letting go. Sure, we look to Chris and Dave [Ancel] for their direction, and they do provide a strong vision while enabling the community to shape its own future. I know that the content has been developed by colleagues, not Dave and Chris saying, 'This is what we're going to do.' We all own the development of where we're heading."

Cavanaugh-Simmons is extremely optimistic about the future and the continuing improvement of Emergent Solutions' Consulting 2.0 model. As the social networking component of the company's utility continues to grow, consultants are enjoying the richness of their Guild community. Their contributions to the wiki give them greater access to the expertise and tools that each of them brings to the table. Says Cavanaugh-Simmons, "We needed something to address a growing global organization, and now we have a great way to share information 24/7. More cocreation is our Holy Grail, and we're excited about that business opportunity with our customers."

Emergent Solutions capitalized on the connections available to every organization—large and small, profit and nonprofit. Although these kinds of organizations vary widely in purpose, customer base, output, structure, composition, and business model, they all have one thing in common: they are nothing without their people. The successful use of social media is not about technology; it's about people. It is about the *in-between*: relationships and connections that catapult ideas, energy, and purpose. What enabled Emergent Solutions' success was its emphasis on leading its team through change in adopting a new way to do their work through social media.

So far, we've discussed the need for organizations to embrace social media, reviewed some of the key social technologies, and looked at multiple ways that organizations can benefit from the use of social media to improve their performance. But how do you begin using these technologies in *your* organization?

Although our research yielded no one way or no single proven tried-and-true method, we have noticed trends in behavior and in the lessons from the companies we examined. In this chapter, we share what we observed about how social media tends to take hold in organizations. We also provide a playbook for gaining adoption in your organization.

Our intention is to help you more easily achieve greater use of social media in your organization. The faster the people in your organization adopt social media (or any change to the way they work), the less productivity you will lose during uncertain times. We do not intend to extol the virtues of one technology, product, or vendor over another. Likewise, we will avoid discussing technology systems, database requirements, or software. Many other books tackle these subjects. Our focus will be on how to change people's attitudes and behaviors in order to implement social media at work most effectively.

As is true of any large, complex, or uncomfortable change, adoption involves attitudinal change. It's not an intellectual decision; rather, it is a personal commitment that sneaks up on you. Unconsciously, people take a belief, a set of assumptions, and a behavior as their own. They will only truly adopt a new mind-set or behavior when they are ready, willing, and able. You can help them get there.

How Social Media Takes Hold

In any evolutionary process, things have a way of unfolding in their own way and in their own time. The emergence of social networking strategies as common behavior is so new, particularly as a lever within organizations, that an understanding of the way it becomes part of an organization's operations is still taking shape. But we have identified common trends in the many examples and experiences of organizations. Some organizations use an "all-hands-on-deck" approach. Top leadership mandates the change, and all facets of the change are implemented at the same time in all geographic locations and all functional groups. The all-hands-on-deck approach is likely to work best in smaller organizations with a workforce that is very homogenous in age and perspectives. We've seen how Emergent Solutions, with its small but globally dispersed Guild and very visionary leaders, has been quite successful in adopting social media using this approach. All-hands-on-deck is also more likely to succeed where the workforce is very tech savvy and hungry for a common infrastructure, process, or method to reduce confusion.

Some organizations use more of a "phased" approach that enables smaller groups in an organization—usually distinct geographies or functional groups—to make the changes at different points in time. The advantage of such an approach is that the organization experiences disruption as smaller "tremors" over time rather than as one major earthquake. A phased implementation allows for learning along the way. Both implementation approaches are viable. Both begin as top-down, leader-sponsored efforts. Each has its advantages and disadvantages.

The alternative to the all-hands-on-deck and the phased approaches is the "bubble-up" or "bottom-up" approach, which is the most common way that social media takes hold in larger organizations. This approach involves three phases: pioneering, exploring, and leveraging. In this natural evolution, a few pioneers begin experimenting, word spreads, curiosity takes hold, and more people explore in their small subgroups. This can occur in the form of clandestine efforts. Early adopters explore with tools familiar to them from outside the organization and with the tools the pioneers provide them inside the organization in beta form. Over time, stories of success promote more experimentation, and a critical mass builds within the organization. By then, executive leadership begins to hear of tangible success stories and feels the pulse of its people. They are clamoring for consistency, direction, and greater leverage of their efforts. This is the time for infrastructure. This is when leaders can offer a recommended set of tools and a home base for activity. Perhaps most important, by this time they have identified the ways that social technologies can truly improve the organization's capability and performance, strategically using them to their advantage.

The all-hands-on-deck, phased, and bubble-up approaches are the most common ways that social media becomes part of an organization's way of life. In any of these approaches, there are opportunities for leaders, human resource managers, or organization development consultants to speed the adoption of social media, accelerating the productivity gain. Although this is new territory, there are many who are forging ahead eagerly.

We have pulled together an aggregate of insights from those embarking on the journey. There are many ways we could have shared this with you. In the end we landed on three groups of findings from our research, and these constitute the playbook.

Our first observations led us to a common *process* for implementing social media. Those who long for a recommended sequential set of activities to facilitate adoption will be pleased to see this basic, step-by-step method. Equally important are *practices*. As you move through the process, *how* you do so has an impact on your success. We discuss many of the human dynamics of adoption that are rooted in change management research and experience. We've incorporated the best practices gathered from our many interviews. Our interviewees have "been there, done that." They've tried, failed, experimented, succeeded, forged new paths, invented new processes, probably cried a few tears, and certainly toasted to some great accomplishments. In addition to the process and practices, we summarize the key lessons that have come from these organizations' experiences. We call these lessons *emerging wisdom*. This wisdom is born from the obstacles that have challenged the social media pioneers. In many cases they have found ways to overcome these challenges, and in some cases, they are still exploring viable solutions. In short, the insights in this guide are not "ours" alone; they are a compilation of the research, risks, experience, and wisdom of many trailblazers. The lessons will continue to unfold as we all gain more experience in this ongoing journey.

The Process

Process activities are high-level tasks you can perform in shaping the progress of social media adoption. We have identified the following process activities:

1. Get intelligence
2. Clarify objectives
3. Design strategies
4. Implement the plan
5. Measure outcomes
6. Leverage learning

It is difficult to describe this process without the practices that must accompany them. We have separated the two in order to force a distinction, but in reality they are inextricable—what we do and how we do it—just as science and art should go hand in hand to create great masterpieces.

Get Intelligence

Perhaps this first step in the process should read "Become intelligent by getting intelligence." Begin your effort armed with information about your environment and your organization. Many strategic planning efforts begin with an environmental scan or SWOT analysis (strengths, weaknesses, opportunities, and threats). In an environmental scan, an organization gathers information about both the external and internal environments so that leaders can make better decisions in the planning process. It is easy to imagine the benefits of gathering intelligence about the external environment. For example, a consumer package goods company, perhaps a cereal company, might study the demographics of potential customers, researching whether it should develop products geared toward the Boomer population or capturing the loyalty of Millennials? The product as well as the marketing campaigns may vary drastically. And as a result, the employees the company hires and the development it provides will differ as well.

Internal environments are just as important. Work911, an online business planning Web site, notes the importance of internal scans and their connection with a systems model: "An internal environmental scan involves looking at the present capabilities of the organization (infrastructure, hardware, personnel, abilities, structure, etc.) and that information can be compared to what the organization will need in the future to achieve its strategic goals."[1]

Here's what we think you should include in your intelligence gathering effort and why. Table 6.1 describes key recommended areas of information you will need to gather about your organization's population and how to use this intelligence in the adoption process.

Clarify Objectives

A little enthusiasm can be dangerous. As more individuals become comfortable with social media, organizations will increasingly begin to investigate its advantages. Often new users' enthusiasm may lead them to adopt strategies that don't necessarily address their true needs. Although we recommend experimentation, we are strong advocates of clarifying the needs of your organization and determining how social media can best propel performance. This is particularly important for organizations that are trying a top-down approach and those that are entering the leveraging phase.

Table 6.1 Social Media Organizational Assessment

Gather intelligence about:	Description:	Use your intelligence to:
Demographic profile	Age, ethnic background, tenure in the company, industry experience	Position communications to have greatest impact, understand motivators, and anticipate resistance accurately.
Social media user profile	Comfort level with social technologies and typical activities related to using it	Determine which social technologies to implement and how to target them.
Readiness for complex change	History of success in large change efforts; change leader capability; level of trust in leaders, technology, and each other; shared view of the need for social media; a commonly understood perception of problems and causes driving the need; an openness to experimentation with new solutions	Emphasize the need for effective change leadership practices, identify and mitigate the greatest risk areas involved in the implementation process, involve key people effectively throughout the effort, plan strategies for building momentum, maintain productivity as change occurs.
Present state of your organizational system	The components and effectiveness of the current organizational system; how work is accomplished and how the organization is designed to sustain performance	Anticipate how the use of social media will change the way the organization will operate; plan for intended and unintended consequences; ascertain a realistic picture of how much "work" will be involved in implementation, what level of social media use you might expect to reach, and the types of metrics you might employ to evaluate successful use.

It is important that your efforts with social media serve your organization's mission and strategic plan. There is always the inherent benefit of adopting social technologies to provide a contemporary climate for Gen X and Y employees. However, you will be mistaken in thinking that the mere existence of social technologies in your organization will enable you to compete successfully with your peers. If you have not tied your social media strategies to your organization's strategic plan, but your competitors have, then you'll lose traction.

An Epicor white paper cited in *CIO* online describes the impact of social media on organizational performance, namely that it brings "capabilities to business users that were not possible previously. These include enabling users to securely... search; enhancing collaboration both internally and with partners, suppliers and customers; boosting the usability of business applications; improving the ability to customize and integrate applications; as well as simplifying application upgrades and maintenance."[2] The strategic value of these capabilities depends on the organization's business strategy. For example, some organizations will want to enhance customer service by empowering employees with the information they need to better address customer questions. Others will wish to bring new products to market faster by improving collaboration between the enterprise and its suppliers, customers, and partners. Each organization will have different objectives for social media to best support their key business strategies.

Two important aspects of clarifying objectives are (1) to articulate how social networking strategies will improve your organization's success and (2) to measure the degree to which you are achieving the desired outcome. These two aspects go hand in hand. (We will cover measurement later in this section.)

One of the best methods for clarifying strategy is the use of the Balanced Scorecard and corresponding strategy map, a method of displaying and communicating an organization's purposeful strategic decisions. Developed by Norton and Kaplan in 1992, the Balanced Scorecard was revolutionary in combining strategy, systems thinking, measurement, and communications.[3] Norton and Kaplan proposed that there was more to measure in organizational strategy than financial outcomes. Because revenue is a lagging indicator, by the time you measure it, it's too late to make critical adjustments to your enterprise's operations. Instead, Norton and Kaplan set forth how three additional perspectives work together to feed the ultimate success of the organization: learning and growth (human, information, and organizational capital), internal processes, and customer. Without conscious and interdependent efforts in each of these areas of the organization, financial performance is limited.

The Balanced Scorecard's strategy map is a summary of the organization's strategy that enables the discussion of how social media will improve each of the four perspectives.[4] The process of creating a strategy map clarifies the objectives of an organization and yields specific metrics for regular tracking. Although there are many ways to capture metrics in a dashboard format, we recommend the Balanced Scorecard process because it focuses on a systems view and is a powerful communication tool. Most important, working with the strategy map enables leaders to see where social media could have a significant impact on organizational performance.

Design Strategies

This is the stage when the intelligence you have gathered, your organization's strategic plan, and your objectives for social media strategies come together. It is the time to put down your well thought out ideas about how to best accelerate the adoption of social media for your organization. Ask yourself the following questions when you design your implementation strategy:

- Given what we know about the audiences in our organization, and given our organization's strategic plan and key objectives, which social media tools can best help us achieve our business strategy? Where will they have the greatest impact? (Consider the five areas we have discussed in previous chapters.)

- Whom will we involve? When and how will we involve them so that we can gain the most commitment?
- What specific training is needed for different groups so that they can use the new tools available to them?
- Where are the best opportunities to gain some quick wins?
- How will we track our progress?
- How will we communicate our success?

In all your planning, just remember that a good strategic plan today is better than a perfect one tomorrow. In other words, it doesn't have to be perfect—it just has to be done. All strategic plans evolve, and so will yours.

Implement the Plan

From a process perspective, this is the easy part. Every organization has implemented changes before. Large corporations have certified project management professionals, for example. Community organizations have the savvy go-to person who always drives home the agreed-on actions. Public sector organizations have policies that give direction and guide able project managers and their teams. During the implementation of your plan, the strategies you have chosen will come to life.

One of the key decision points during implementation is the selection of business partners, if you opt to work with them. These are likely to be software and service providers as well as consulting firms. They are critical to the success of your efforts, and selecting them should involve more than an analysis of their technical solution. Many tangible and intangible factors need to be considered in your decision. According to Cavanaugh-Simmons, Emergent Solutions' partner was chosen because it had the vision and passion about social technology that could pull Emergent Solutions toward its own ultimate goals. Here is a simple list of considerations to help you with your decision, organized into the following categories: experience, capability, and fit.

EXPERIENCE

- What is the prospective partner's experience with social media solutions?
- What is its experience implementing within your industry or type of organization?

CAPABILITY

- How well can the prospective partner integrate or dovetail with your current technology solutions?
- Are its systems secure? Will those systems work within your firewall?
- What is its data storage, backup, and recovery strategy?
- Does it have a robust search capability to mine for information effectively?
- What is the prospective partner's plan for transferring knowledge and expertise to your own employees?
- How do its solutions and technical infrastructure grow and change as your organization implements, learns, and improves the social technology strategy over time?
- What is your sense of partnership with this company? Do you have a good "gut feeling" about it? Do you feel that its people understand what you are trying to accomplish, your hopes, and your unique challenges?

- How does the company partner with its customers? How well does it recognize your organization's objectives, people, and culture?
- What is its vision of social media and social computing technology? What opportunities does the company see in the future, and how is it prepared to become a key player?
- Is the prospective partner a good cultural fit for your organization?

Another key decision to include in your plan relates to determining the best way to prepare the organization's members to contribute using your social media tools. Pull out your social media user profile (the one in the social media assessment you conducted earlier, using Table 6.1) to determine the kind of training needed for different groups in your organization. Some employees will first need to become aware of social media tools, how they are used, and the benefits they offer. Others may simply need to become familiarized with the particular tools you are providing. Other employees may be resistant or fearful. Your training programs double as excellent communication strategies, enabling you to share your vision and expectations and to solicit input from organizational members. This exchange is critical for building trust and preparing users to embrace and begin using social media quickly.

Measure Impact

You will need to measure the impact of your social media implementation efforts in terms of your organization's performance as well as organizational health. Three metric categories come into play:

- Project implementation: Are we implementing the social media plan we designed?
- Organizational design: Is our use of social media helping us achieve our organization's strategy and key objectives?
- Output: Is our new way of working (or our new organizational system) producing the output we require?

Often organizations measure only the first category. Managers fill status reports with spreadsheets, create work breakdown structures, color in red-yellow-green stoplight indicators, and check off milestones. Rarely, however, do leaders and teams tie their initiatives clearly to the organization's strategic plan (if indeed there is one). They overlook determining how the organization should operate, as a system, to realize that strategic plan and produce desired results. Not to mention, leaders and teams often fail to integrate their actions with the measurement of organizational output in a cause-and-effect way. This is why the Balanced Scorecard is so valuable—it creates a view of the organization as a system.

At Genentech Corporation, Omar Nielsen, senior manager for emerging technologies, and Don Kraft, director of learning and organization development, have been using social media in a variety of ways. Both emphasize that real results may take some time to show themselves. They note that as groups form new online social communities, true adoption occurs gradually. Group members need time to gel as a community and to ease into their own cadence of interaction. Consequently, Nielsen cautions, "Often it may take a group twelve to eighteen months to really hum, producing results that move their efforts ahead in huge ways. Expect that your metrics may show solid improvement a year down the line."

Leverage Learning

The final activity in our process is to reapply the learning that has taken place. True learning typically involves experience, reflection, analysis, insight, and reapplication in another itera-tion. This step in the process serves as a placeholder allowing everyone to pause, reflect, learn, and reapply as activities are revisited and efforts move forward. This is particularly useful for what we call the phased approaches and when planning specific initiatives as pilots or proof points, as we've seen with Cisco's CDO training (discussed in Chapter Four).

The Practices

Practices in our adoption guide are critical. Without them, processes could be mistaken as merely business models or light methodologies. We stated previously that the practices we include here are drawn from libraries of research regarding effective change leadership and implementation skills, many years assisting leaders and teams to shape effective organizations, and recent experiences and collective learning from those who are blazing the way for others to capitalize on social media in organizations. If the process is the "what" to do, the practices are "how" to do it.

The "how," however, is not a trivial matter and often involves skills that some find intuitive. It is difficult to make this kind of tacit knowledge explicit. Yet, we have attempted to do so in describing these practices and associated activities. Nevertheless, all practices should be experimented with, reflected on, and repeated for improved learning. Of course, one can practice, practice, and practice oneself into a habit of reaching disastrous outcomes. Breaking out of these nonproductive practices requires the courage to do things differently than normal and bucking business-as-usual behaviors.

Again, the four practices we discuss here are rooted in change management research. Using social media at work can be a new skill for some and may entail substantial organizational change. Much confusion, frustration, and doubt characterizes the ambiguous phase between the old status quo and new modus operandi. People are unsure of the way to behave because their regular methods for accomplishing work are disrupted. They may need to learn new processes, use new tools, gain new skills, and forge new relationships. During this transition, organizational productivity drops while team members spend energy in resisting and experimenting at the expense of their regular activities. The key is to help individuals and communities cope with the loss of their familiar way of operating and embrace the new paradigm as quickly as possible, reducing the length of uncertainty and the severity of productivity loss.

In our experience, four vital practices are powerful yet simple ways to help organizations implement social media successfully, maintaining performance and employee commitment:

1. Involve others for commitment
2. Communicate to build trust
3. Work the system
4. Generate momentum

Involve Others for Commitment

Organizational change can't happen without achieving a critical mass of commitment. For social media implementation efforts to succeed, we've found that the following considerations are critical in securing mindshare.

Identify Stakeholders. Stakeholders are the people who will be affected by the use of new social media in your organization— that is, they have a "stake" in the success (or failure) of the adoption. Underlying the need to identify stakeholders is the fact that they may have different perspectives on the use of social technologies, particularly when it will disrupt the regular methods of accomplishing work or relating with colleagues. For example, we can make assumptions about the likely responses of different generational perspectives. Gen Yers, already comfortable with technology, may be ready and willing to embrace social media, whereas Traditionalists may not understand how a wiki could ever replace sketching out ideas on the back of a napkin over a good cup of coffee. Identifying stakeholders is the first step in planning your involvement strategies appropriately. You will want to involve various stakeholders in the planning and implementation so that they understand how social technology can help them with their personal effectiveness as well as increase organizational effectiveness. Use your demographic profile (from the organizational assessment in Table 6.1) to involve a range of stakeholders. When they participate, they get "skin in the game" and have a sense of ownership and contribution. This leads to greater commitment, and commitment is critical to maintaining momentum for the adoption effort.

Secure Sponsorship. Sponsorship is a crucial ingredient in adoption practices. Sponsors are leaders with a particular role to play in any adoption effort. They publicly pledge their support, advocate among power bases in an organization, remove barriers to success, provide resources, and make key decisions regarding allocation of budget, headcount, and materials. Most important, they underscore the organization's strategic direction so that social media can fuel organizational success.

Ideally, a strong sponsor steps forward at the onset of the adoption effort. Dave Simpson, a consultant in the Guild at Emergent Solutions, commented on the power of strong sponsorship during the company's move to social technologies: "Having strong leadership was key. Right from the beginning Chris and Dave [Ancel] set the tone by letting us know their vision for how this new way of collaborating would enable us to be more effective and ease some of the biggest challenges the consultants were facing." However, as noted in our discussion of the bubble-up approach, sponsorship may come at a later iteration of the process, once a critical mass has seen success with the new technologies and behaviors.

Use Connectors, Mavens, and Salespeople. Among your many stakeholders are particularly gifted people who greatly assist the adoption effort. In his book *The Tipping Point*, Malcolm Gladwell describes why some changes spread with viral speed and reach, whereas others tucker out.[5] The key to this phenomenon, what Gladwell labels the tipping point, is characterized by the context, the idea, and the involvement of certain types of people: what he calls Connectors, Salespeople, and Mavens.

Connectors are central to the success of viral messages because they are the hubs of human networks. These socially adept people seem to know everyone, and they have a knack for bringing people together. Connectors are likely to have more than two hundred "friends" on Facebook or LinkedIn. You need Connectors to spread the good word and bring your message of the benefit of social media to the masses in your organization.

Mavens may not have the vast number of friends that Connectors do, but they are seen as helpful teachers with information they gladly share with no ulterior motive or hidden agenda. They have the trust of their colleagues, and they are open minded and willing to add new knowledge to their repertoire. Mavens are likely to contribute valuable content to a wiki, and will be great advocates of the value of social media.

You also need Salespeople: they have the gift of persuasion. They will take the doubtful team member and craft an argument that will turn the tide, all with a pleasant smile that leaves the other with a "Gosh, he's a nice guy" conclusion. You need Salespeople to help carry the success stories to executive leaders. They will be the ones who can secure the IT department's support, strike the best deal with your vendor, and help make the case for infrastructure when you arrive at the leveraging phase.

Communicate to Build Trust

As organizational commitment begins to increase, it is important to sustain the momentum and build trust through effective communication. People hate unexpected silence. Silence during your adoption effort can leave a dangerous void. In the absence of information, your audience will be compelled to fill the void with rumors, conjecture, and their creative stories—regardless of any resemblance to fact. Unless extremely high trust already permeates your organization at every level, don't let your adoption fall victim to someone else's story; be sure to give everyone the real one. This is where trust begins, and you need a lot of organizational trust when you inform people that some of their relationships, processes, and tools are changing. Here are some ideas to keep in mind.

Engage Through Targeted Messages. Pull out the demographic profile you created during your organizational assessment (see Table 6.1) and look at it with a variety of lenses. What distinguishes your audience most? Is it functional culture? Is it regional norms? One lens that is critical to the adoption of social media reveals insights about generational differences. How homogenous is your organization, or, conversely, how diverse? These are important considerations when crafting your communications plan and messages. If you have a diverse organization, a one-size-fits-all message will fall on a lot of deaf ears. Gen Yers might take to an "it's cool; we're contemporary" message, but this won't play with Traditionalists. They may like to hear how these new strategies will impact the bottom line and increase productivity.

Another lens may show gender differences. For example, one study suggests that women in general have a different motivation from men for engaging in social networking—they do it t build relationships rather than transact.[6] This information can be used to create more targeted explanations of the value of social media in communications.

Another important aspect of your communication plan is that it should be two-way in nature. This is the time to hear the perspectives of your various stakeholder generations and functional groups. Their comments are useful to confirm your direction and will illuminate real risks and obstacles. They're also likely to have the best solutions to those obstacles.

Create "Sticky" Messages. As we all know, communication can affect perceptions, biases, and ultimately trust. Conveying the right messages is important. However, it's equally important to ensure that people *remember* those messages. In the case of social media, positive messages about its utility need to outlive any negative ones people may receive. In *Made to Stick*, Chip and Dan Heath focus on what makes messages "sticky" and explain the objective of their work: "Our interest is in how effective ideas are constructed—what makes some ideas stick and others disappear."[7] The Heaths discuss how urban legends travel the globe as fact. They reveal six principles they have found to be common in sticky ideas:

1. Simplicity: The best ideas are both profound and simple. Like parables, these short messages carry long-term meaning.

2. Unexpectedness: Be bold and spontaneous. The element of surprise grabs interest.

3. Concreteness: Don't forget to use images. A picture really is worth a thousand words, and a graphic description gives shape and texture to abstract ideas.

4. Credibility: Give people the chance to try out your idea for themselves. Taste-testing helps them in deciding whether to buy into your idea.

5. Emotions: Mathematician Blaise Pascal observed, "The heart has arguments with which the logic of the mind is not acquainted." Despite our most rational thinking, we can't ignore our gut feelings. Craft a message that tugs at the heart-strings of others.

6. Stories: We all remember a good story. Stories give context to an idea with a chain of events and interesting characters. Good stories have long lives and travel far. Tell stories to your audience that are too good to keep to themselves.

We like the "sticky six" because they make common sense. They require no special training and no marketing credentials. As the Heaths put it, "There are no licensed stickologists." [8] Nevertheless, like most principles in adopting change, these make sense but are less commonly practiced. Combine a well-crafted, sticky message with a Connector, Maven, and Salesperson on your side, and you have a great start at spreading the news of how social media will improve your organization's capability and performance.

Shout Success from the Mountaintops. When working on the adoption of social networking strategies, this not the time for humility. As one of the key elements of stickiness, your story is what will travel to distant corners of the organization. Create the buzz. The social system, otherwise known as the grapevine, will latch onto it, enabled by your new communication tools. The interim successes and the brave explorers must be spotlighted for the hesitant to see. Without this reinforcement, these early adopters remain unrewarded, and the others have nothing to talk about at the watercooler, on the web conference, or on their blog.

Work the System

Now that you are more aware of the natural evolution of social media in your organization, it's useful to see the big picture of how organizations operate. Your organization is in motion, and you will be rattling the status quo with the use of social media. Organizations of all kinds are open systems. They are not self-contained. They interact with the environment beyond their four walls. They pull from their environment needed inputs and bring them into their organizational system—their day-to-day operation—to create products and services. For example, organizations listen to customer needs, obtain resources from suppliers, form partnerships, have a physical and brand presence in the marketplace, and support customers after the sale.

Recognizing your organization as an open system reminds you that what happens *inside* your organization will likely show up *outside*, and vice versa. The boundary that you imagine separating your organization from the outside world is really a transparent film, and a flimsy one at that. Employees share frustrations with their friends—and the long-term effect of that is the inability to attract and retain the best employees. Customers share bad experiences—and the long-term effect of that is decreased brand loyalty and the inability to forge strategic partnerships. You get the picture.

Of course, the way your enterprise works internally is also systemic. If you want to change employees' priorities, you must educate them, enable them with the right tools, and reward them appropriately. Any one of these without the others is futile. Likewise, to speed a product to market you must hire the right designers, ensure that your manufacturing process is up-to-date, and partner with the right distributors. Any one of these without the other will not place you on the shelf first.

It is critical to have an understanding of organizational dynamics and of the specific dynamics of your organizational world as you attempt to make any complex change, particularly if you desire successful adoption of social media strategies. Knowing the makeup of your organizational system enables you to identify how your strategies are likely to affect the operational components of your enterprise and the resulting output you create. More important, systems thinking informs the actions you must take to align the components for sustained capability and performance. If you want people to use social media in their work, you must integrate it into your organization's system effectively. You must educate employees of its value, provide easy access to tools, reinforce social media as part of your work process, and reward those who contribute to and collaborate with these tools.

The following are some suggestions for integrating social media into the dynamics of your organizational system.

Spell Out New Operating Norms. Cavanaugh-Simmons of Emergent Solutions described one of the biggest challenges the company's extended team of consultants experienced when they implemented a wiki as their primary collaboration tool. "One thing we didn't anticipate was how our working norms would change. The way we've typically divvied up work, tracked our progress, and improved iterations turned out to be unnecessary. We quickly realized we had to make explicit our new process, new tools, and new working norms." Cavanaugh-Simmons saw how the organization's daily operating system was tweaked. The team needed to understand that they were riding a new bike, and Cavanaugh-Simmons needed to ensure that the wheels were true and that the system was in alignment. Because social technologies change the way people work together, adjustments to the alignment are often needed, and without the explicit recognition of how work will get done, employees will be frustrated with new tools that don't match the old processes and norms they stubbornly maintain.

Consider Unintended Consequences. One of the most common unintended consequences of the adoption of social media is the alienation of a segment of your organization's population. This is a difficult situation to face when the intent of the social technologies is to create a more cohesive workforce. Resistance is common, particularly among those who feel threatened by new ways of working or new information channels. Consider the senior manager who has worked hard to build political alliances, gain industry experience, and amass a team of individuals who look to him for expertise and guidance. A new wiki, discussion forum, and industry social network suddenly enables newer staff to find answers without him, and to learn more from their peers in other groups. Although he may acknowledge that the increase in knowledge is good for his team's productivity, the loss of informal power may lead him to feel less valuable to his team and the organization. He may begin to subvert efforts to capitalize on social networking, limit his team, or decide to take his years of experience and knowledge to another organization.

This is just one of many unintended consequences that should be considered. Imagine the working future state of your organization. Where will life be most different? What negative implications could social media have? To prevent unintended consequences, anticipate them and incorporate specific activities into your plan that will create the organization you want. All is not in the hands of fate: you can take action to create the future.

Reinforce Movement. If the manager we described in the previous scenario turns the corner and avails himself of the same social networking tools, he too will benefit from increased knowledge, particularly if his mature network joins him online as well. In fact, he can become a great contributor to the social network, in turn, boosting his sense of value and self-worth. This is the opportunity to reinforce his actions in adopting the new technology and behaviors. He can become an example, a story to shout out from the mountaintop. He is particularly useful within the community of his peers who may still be resistant. Pair him up with a peer who does not see value in social media, and allow him to make the case for you. If he's a Maven or a Salesperson, he will serve as an effective advocate.

Generate Momentum

Some say that healthy organizational systems are always directional—they are going somewhere. From a cultural perspective, changing direction or accelerating a desired change requires momentum. Depending on the size of your organization and also on the scale of the desired change, momentum can be difficult to obtain. But huge increases in momentum do not always require proportional efforts—small and simple actions can create great results. The following are some ideas to help in this process.

Find a Gardener. We touched on this at the beginning of the chapter. A vegetable garden doesn't do well if left untended. But with a little fertilizer, pruning, watering, and perhaps some tender loving care, seedlings will eventually bear good fruit. If you begin a relationship with readers by writing a blog, you must continually come back to share your thoughts. Unless you provide a consistent stream of commentary, readers will lose interest in favor of other, more compelling information. Marty Fahncke, author and Internet marketing specialist, recommends that once you start, you should blog regularly, perhaps every two weeks.[9] Others recommend different intervals, but the trend is clear: you must put in regular attention to cultivate your social network. If you create content, you must create it regularly to maintain momentum.

In addition to a consistent stream of new information, a critical role is needed behind the scenes. Greg Pope of Questionmark insisted, "You need to put someone in charge—not of the content—but of the maintenance and membership support." Cavanaugh-Simmons explained, "One of the best things we did was to ask Claudia to look after the site. We needed a gardener, and she's been great at keeping the wiki well organized." Ongoing maintenance is a major obstacle to success. It is important for information to be located in the optimal place, where members of a community can search for information, contribute content, and comment on others' thoughts easily. The gardener is the one who ensures that the tools you use are kept up-to-date, accessible, and most useful.

Create Small Wins and Proof Points. In concert with the bubble-up approach, the pioneers and early adopters will be forging ahead, experimenting and generating small successes. Exploit this creative energy and experience by finding an opportunity for a small success that addresses an important organizational issue or long-standing desire. The older generations will require proof points and visible results before investing time, energy, and budget in social media strategies. You have to offer them evidence. Be smart about selecting opportunities for strong wins, and offer them to your early adopters.

At Intel, Laurie Buczek, the social computing program manager, was thrilled to connect with Steve Snyder, information technology (IT) program manager. Snyder saw the power of using social media to promote the value of "green" work practices. The cost savings in IT was one opportunity, but Snyder had the vision of employees sharing their green strategies with each other and bringing new ideas from their personal lives into their work lives. The potential was huge, and Snyder sought Buczek's support in using social media for the effort. Buczek was eager to help: "Steve had a perfect business case. We're excited to see how we can promote these new behaviors across Intel with the help of social computing technologies."

Burn the Ships If Necessary. We teach our organizations to move slowly. Humans are intelligent beings, and they learn quickly. Everyone knows the familiar scene of a parent at the dinner table telling her child for the eighth time, "That's it, kiddo—I'm not going to say it again. This is your last chance. Eat your peas. I mean it, now; I'm not kidding . . ." This child knows there are at least a few more "last chances" left. In organizations, we're even smarter. After many stalled initiatives, abandoned projects, and mouse pads imprinted with last year's campaign, employees know when to adopt the attitude, "If I just wait a little longer to get on board, this too shall pass, and it will be business as usual again."

Hernando Cortés, Spanish explorer, was a change leader ahead of his time. After landing in Veracruz, Mexico, his four hundred men were reluctant to overthrow the Aztecs. The story of his unique way of motivating his crew has been told repeatedly—a truly sticky message. A Thinkquest article on the Aztec conquest describes it this way: "Unhappiness and unrest among his force caused Cortés to burn the ships in which the Spaniards had arrived, thus ensuring conquest as the only means of long-term survival."[10] The lesson is clear for change leaders. At some point, there can be no turning back. It may sound drastic but can work well when used wisely. Cavanaugh-Simmons archived all projects developed using Emergent Solutions' previous tool. The wiki is now the only structure available to employees. After you have created enough "pull" by making the shift to social media strategies irresistible, you may have to switch to a "push" method by abolishing the old structures and leaving your employees no other choice but to join the organization in moving forward.

Table 6.2 summarizes the practices and associated activities we've discussed in this section.

Table 6.2 Key Practices for Implementing Social Media

Practices	Activities
Involve others for commitment	• Identify stakeholders • Secure sponsorship • Use Connectors, Mavens, and Salespeople
Communicate to build trust	• Engage through targeted messages • Create "sticky" ideas • Shout success from the mountaintops
Work the system	• Spell out new operating norms • Consider unintended consequences • Reinforce movement
Generate momentum	• Find a gardener • Create small wins and proof points • Burn the ships if necessary

Emerging Wisdom

One can consider wisdom as "knowledge applied well." With respect to using social media in organizations, we'd like to propose that wisdom consists of the appropriate integration of processes and practices—the comingling of just the right quantities of all the ingredients we have talked about in this chapter, creating magic in terms of widespread adoption of social media within your organization.

We can't emphasize strongly enough that there will be differences in how and to what degree social media is implemented in every organization. However, we do believe there are at least a few guiding principles that can help you along the way. Author, professor, and consultant Marshall Goldsmith says, "A wise person learns from experience—a wiser person learns from someone else's experience."[11] Beyond the processes and practices we've already discussed, here are a few more tidbits of wisdom passed on to us by leaders we've interviewed. Some gained these pearls through their successes, and others through their "mistakes," but however the lessons were learned, the wisdom is now yours to use!

Consider Privacy and Access Issues

Be sure to consider the right technology platform with the right security for your needs. We've seen that members of the organization are looking for safe and secure ways to share openly. If they have a nagging concern that their data or ideas may be seen by unintended audiences, they will hold back their contributions. This defeats the power of the social media tools. It is critical to engage your IT group or technology provider in a clear conversation about your organization's privacy needs.

Share Clear Policies

Because the use of social media may involve a new set of behaviors, organizations should make their expectations clear. We say this with caution because a central premise of sharing with social media is the ability to accomplish more with a free exchange of knowledge, ideas, and resources. But employees, volunteers, and community members will appreciate knowing the boundaries for use. Creating the right policies with regard to use, scope of access, and privacy will also significantly influence the success of your efforts in implementing social media. Of course, policies can change over time, but be sure you have them! A good company policy for participation in social media will cover many, if not all, of the following topics:

- Which social media the policy applies to (for example, blogs, wikis, forums, and other multimedia)
- Subject matter covered (products, customers, competitive information, and so on)
- How company use of social media may or may not relate to use of social media outside the company
- Acceptable and unacceptable uses and content
- Confidentiality of certain information about employees, the company, customers, marketing or acquisition activities, unannounced products, and so on
- Encouragement of courtesy and respect
- Whether anonymous use is acceptable or not (one large Silicon Valley biotech has a "no anonymous blog posts" policy, which encourages courtesy, thoughtfulness, and accountability)
- Respect for copyrights
- When one can speak for the company and when one cannot

- Responsible use of company resources
- Where to go for help, questions, or more information (for example, the legal department, one's manager, or corporate communications)

Set the Tone

In addition to documented policies, there is an intangible energy to social communities in organizations; each has its own tone and personality. As you initiate effective social communities, be sure to set the tone you seek. The tone reinforces the behaviors of the community members. Let the purpose of the community guide the tone. Is the community about exchanging valuable knowledge and information with those who need it? Then you might expect a lot of questions and quick replies with data, information, resources, and referrals. Is the community about innovation and development? Then you want participants to share big ideas and outlandish goals, and you want them to pair unlikely bits of information without the fear of looking foolish.

Don Kraft, director of learning and organization development at Genentech, helped shape the tone of the social networking sites used in the company's learning solutions: "Our intent is to enhance learning, so I encourage each of our community managers to really push the envelope in the discussions with participants. This way they really move the learning forward in meaningful ways. They know that's expected of them, and the participants know they are expected to contribute to provocative and challenging debate."

In addition to the social media components you chose to include, consider design as well—the look and feel of your site. Color, fonts, graphics, the amount of text in relation to white space—all these play an important role in setting the proper tone for your community. If you are partnering with a vendor, ensure that it knows the tone you are trying to set. If you are using a public tool, this task will fall to you.

Choose the Appropriate Technology

Technology isn't the most important consideration, but you do need to give it some thought. Be sure to select technology platforms and vehicles that are both scalable (extendable with increasing use of social media in your organization) and interoperable (integrated with other technology you already use or will use in the future). You will need some server space and decent software. Once you decide on the basics, the technology you can leverage or apply is limitless—literally! Do your homework—but know when to avoid "analysis paralysis" and to act with decisiveness in implementing *something* (which is always preferable to nothing). As technologist Ben Katz of the simulation maker Enspire says, "Your employees already have experience with social media tools.... So just find out and use what your employees already enjoy, rather than pushing them in another direction."

Focus on the Value Proposition

A reason for using social media must exist, and that reason must be widely known and shared. It is too difficult to mandate the use of social media if it does not truly serve a good purpose. Although a little pushing is sometimes needed, the *pull* of a more effective team, an easier job, a brighter future is always more enticing. Spread the word about the value early in your effort, and remind everyone often.

As noted in the process step of clarifying objectives, the value proposition should be tied to your strategies. The value proposition can be organizational at first, but it must eventually be internalized individually. Allow room for the transition to occur, knowing that everyone will adopt at his or her own rate—and some will not adopt at all. In one firm, the senior executives of a particular business unit sponsored the implementation of social media, but rarely used it themselves. All kinds of efforts and strategies were used to encourage experimentation and use. Finally, the executives determined that the value of social media in their organization was more operational in nature and did not necessarily require executive involvement. That worked for their firm, and the social media is still in widespread use throughout the organization. This strategy might not work in another firm or situation, but the message is this: evaluate the value proposition, and do it early. Tie it to your strategic plan and tie it to the needs of your people. The sooner the better.

Don't Let Your Checkbook Rule

You don't need to spend a lot of money to begin leveraging the power of social media (but you can if you like!). Ginny Brady, a volunteer on the board of directors for UFirst Federal Credit Union in New York, started a public blog on a shoestring. It's one of the first of its kind in the entire credit union industry. The blog, called The Boardcast (http://www.theboardcast.net) has become an essential tool in creating a connection between the credit union and its local community. In Ginny's mind, the small amount of investment has yielded tremendous dividends for her organization and the credit union movement in her region. Ginny focused her efforts on structure, design, content, and monitoring. She started small, but traffic has grown quickly. She learned that community building is the name of the game. It was the ideal value proposition for UFirst Federal Credit Union.

Remember the "Social" in Social Media

According to Eugene Kim of Blue Oxen, a collaborative consulting company, social media "helps people remember that being social has important effects on trust, communication,

strengthening relationships, learning, and knowledge sharing."
Remembering this raison d'être will help you avoid the mistake of
setting unrealistic adoption goals. Kim thinks of social networking as a way to show the aliveness of an organization as though it
had a discernible pulse.

The Boy Scouts of America (BSA) shares his point of view.
Celebrating its hundredth anniversary in 2010, the BSA turned
to social networking to get the word out about its celebra-
tion among its membership and to generate buzz. Using its
online social networking community called My Scouting, BSA
has quickly galvanized thousands of members to establish a
foundation for communication and collaboration—the pulse of
the movement—effectively organizing and publicizing its 2010
anniversary festivities.

Don't Overwhelm People with Information

Every day we are bombarded with a glut of information. It comes
at us from every direction. We all must avoid contributing to
the modern problem of information overload. If left unchecked,
social media can become just another source of "information
noise." Kim of Blue Oxen admits that this is a problem: "We are
just learning how to address this right now." One way he suggests
to help turn information overload into meaningful insight is to
control the delivery channel. Text message, TV, radio, Twitter,
newspaper, online magazine—each of these channels pumps
information out. Just because more channels carry your message
does not mean that more insight is gained. Sometimes less is more.
Choose the channel that best grabs your audience. Another way
is just to remember that information filtering on the part of the
receiver is perfectly fine: "Sometimes an armchair coach is better
than the real one. They have the advantage of less information."
Says Blake Bush, VP of multimedia at Enspire, "Use it [social
media] because people enjoy it, not simply because everyone's

doing it." That's key. When employees enjoy it and see how it helps them to be more productive, they'll pay attention.

The playbook we've outlined in this chapter is a useful resource for process, practices, and emerging wisdom, but it can't provide every answer. There is no substitute for trial, learning, and improving the next trial. Intel is one company that has been using social media internally for quite some time. We see Intel entering the third phase of the bubble-up process: leveraging. Its workforce has gained a lot of experience and confidence in working with social media tools, and the company's job now is to enable employees to access and use these tools as effectively as possible.

Trailblazer—Intel Discovers Its Playbook

Steve Snyder, program manager for Intel's IT organization, was coordinating the company's green initiative as part of Intel's effort to improve corporate sustainability. He knew that the key was gaining the commitment to act among Intel's more than eighty thousand employees, but wondered how to promote a "green mind-set" across the global workforce. As a user of social media himself, Snyder instinctively turned to Laurie Buczek, Intel's social media program manager, to brainstorm.

Laurie Buczek has the responsibility of cultivating social media at Intel "for our employees to use as the way to transform the way we collaborate and connect and communicate today. I'm only focused on how do we do this right on the inside."

Intel is the world's largest semiconductor company, with a global employee population. Social media has become an integral part of its operations. Because teamwork and innovation are core values, the company fosters the freedom for employees to use this media to their advantage. Intel experienced the bubbling up of social media when its first

TRAILBLAZER

innovators, initially motivated by the "cool" factor, began sharing information with each other through blogs and discussion forums in 2004 and wikis in 2005. Today, every employee, executive, or group can have his or her own blog, discussion forums, or wiki.

Intel uses the term "social computing" to characterize its social media, referring to all social collaboration tools, such as blogs, wikis, streaming media, and microblogging. As Intel began to explore social computing, it uncovered a number of environmental pressures driving internal adoption, including external "consumerization" of social media. Citing the prolific use of these tools outside the work environment, the company recognized the inevitable spillover into internal work environments. No longer is the IT department offering the latest and greatest technology to its people—now it's the reverse. Employees are finding open source software "out there" and introducing it to others internally. Consequently, IT devotes tremendous energy to providing a safe and secure environment for employees to access sensitive information and collaborate freely without fear of competitive sabotage.

Another factor driving social media adoption at Intel is the blend of all four generations in the workforce. Buczek has found that if social computing tools are not provided to Millennial employees, they very quickly disengage and leave for other companies where such tools are more readily available.

Moreover, in the years 2012 to 2014, Intel's Baby Boomers will begin to retire in serious numbers. To date there is no proven method of capturing the knowledge that will walk out the door with them. By leveraging social media, Intel is hoping to find a better way to retain some of this corporate memory—the rationale for decisions, the historical context, and the debates that led to key business strategies.

These drivers have given Intel impetus to shape the next phase of its social computing tools—highly modular architecture that integrates with key office productivity applications, a central portal, and a robust intranet search engine. It has launched new profiles in social networking, encouraged the use of a microblog for status updates, and provided the ability for employees to create their own virtual communities with blogging and wiki functionality.

Such capability is becoming essential during the recruiting and on-boarding process. As we saw in Chapter Five, in 2009, Intel declared a goal to significantly improve the integration of new hires by year end. Social media tools assisted in this process by giving potential recruits a sense that they could start contributing, adding value, and building relationships immediately upon matriculation. Early on, for example, one college intern at Intel's Folsom facility in California sought out the community of other interns. They all tried to connect using e-mail, but soon opted for social networking tools to help them form relationships and plan activities outside of work.

Buczek also tells of a new hire who had not yet established relationships within the company and who was looking for resources and expertise. His manager told him to "talk to Laurie Buczek," but he had no way of knowing who she was or how she could help. Consequently, Intel is working to enhance the corporate phonebook with new social networking features, such as personal profiles, so that people get to know "who's who" when connecting. Employees will be able to add their photo, experiences, interests, and additional information they think is valuable to share with colleagues. This conscious use of social media is paying off for employee integration, as demonstrated through positive internal metrics and new-hire feedback.

TRAILBLAZER

Social computing technologies play a key role in Intel's talent management strategies as well. As a global company, Intel has no central data repository to help identify employee skills, source or provide mentoring, or support career development. Critical knowledge is often hidden in silos. One sales team conducted a study and found that it can take several hours per week per sales rep to find the right information for customers. The cost in lost opportunity, efficiency, and potential revenue is significant. Consequently, Intel is tapping the power of social media to combat this issue.

Many Intel engineers also face major challenges in virtual collaboration and teaming. For example, Intel uses a "follow the sun" model in which work happens twenty-four hours a day and is handed off from one geographic region to another. This model works, but asynchronous collaboration has been difficult. Engineers wanted better ways to collaborate over time, particularly when using multiple authors to contribute to engineering designs. They also wanted to better capture the train of thought as conversations progressed. With discussion forums and wikis, engineers can now capture ideas as they unfold, track historical information, and collaborate without losing any one of the day's twenty-four hours.

Social media use has also resulted in greater trust; there isn't much "face time" at Intel, and social media has helped fill the void. Buczek's next strategy is to consolidate social computing technologies into a "one-stop shop"—one core knowledge portal on Intel's intranet, consolidating all social media sources on a single screen. All employees will know where to go to initiate the use of a social computing tool or to find information through the tools. In addition, Buczek imagines that soon employees will capture brilliant ideas at their desk and use streaming media to create and publish videos to share with others—accessible through the centralized portal, of course.

Yet, as always, challenges persist. Buczek describes one challenge as the "scary software" syndrome. Some leaders and employees are scared of social media because they feel that it distracts employees from their work; they ask, "When are you going to do your real job?" or "Will it hinder productivity?" Buczek overcomes this through education, showing how blogs can replace e-mail to a specific distribution list, facilitating more efficient dissemination of ideas. She also suggests finding business problems that social tools can help solve, conducting proofs of concept, and inviting both skeptics and avid users to provide feedback and learn from history. According to Buczek, Intel recognizes that breaking down silos and sharing information involves changing the culture. Because of this challenge, it constantly searches for new ways to incent and reward collaboration from the top down. As Buczek explains, "Some leaders want to immediately shut down this kind of exchange; however, we believe that you need to engage in it and help shape the conversation. At Intel there is no anonymity in electronic communications. The transparency of the communications helps employees feel ownership in the company, and they feel they have the right to voice their opinion. Their voices have the potential to shape executive actions."

Buczek summarizes Intel's learnings as follows:

- Don't merely apply social media tools over existing organizational silos; if you do, you won't achieve what you want from these tools. You must break down the silos in the process.
- "The train is coming"; there is no stopping the proliferation of electronic tools to help people get connected and

TRAILBLAZER

TRAILBLAZER

remain connected. "Consumerization" of social media is here to stay for the foreseeable future.

- IT departments need to act quickly, or they should be prepared to do a lot of work later.

- Allow grassroots efforts to happen. Enable innovation to occur in a managed way. For mass adoption you need executive buy-in to transform the way work is done. Ideally executives will say, "We are going to transform the way we work!"

- With regard to blogs, allow all employees to have their own blog. This gives them a voice—a means of contributing their knowledge, their experience, and their point of view.

- An important strategy is to integrate social media tools into business processes so that they become the way to accomplish work. Embed them so that employees trip over them as they do their work.

- Enable both early and late adopters to remain in their respective comfort zones. Don't push dramatic changes at one time. Ease people over to the new tools. For example, allow those who don't yet want to leave e-mail to contribute to a blog or forum by clicking a link within their e-mail.

- The number-one success factor remains ease of use. Conduct usability studies that involve end users and gather their feedback. Do not bring a tool in just because it looks good on paper; you need to test it with employees. Employees expect a certain level of functionality from the tools they use; consequently, internal tools need to have the same or better functionality than the ones they use externally. The bar has been set by the consumer tools available outside the company.

Clearly, Intel sees social computing technologies as a key enabler of business performance. It has committed to integrating social computing technology where it can have the greatest impact. The additional transparency this brings the organization is keeping employees engaged and is enabling innovation for sustained success.

Your Own Discovery

Emergent Solutions and Intel have different kinds of organizations with different issues. As they use social media in their organizations, they are blazing a trail for others. As you embark on the implementation of social media tools in your organization, just remember that you know your industry best. You know the norms that guide your organization's everyday behavior. You know the challenges in your operation, and the history of legacy implementations—truths and myths. There is no way to capture your knowledge and insights in broad general statements for everyone, but remember to add them to the process, practices, and emerging wisdom, and let them serve you well. As Eugene Kim of collaborative consulting firm Blue Oxen advises, "Don't be afraid to play and experiment. Remember that we are all humans. Great organizations do that well." Customize the processes and practices into wisdom for your own situation and then be sure to share the wealth by helping others in their journey. As they say, it may not be easy, but it will be well worth the effort!

Join the Conversation

Connect with others who, like you, are exploring, experimenting, and pioneering the use of social media to propel organizational performance. Go to www.socialmediaatwork-connection.com to ask your questions, learn what others are doing, and add your insights to the conversation. This chapter raises the following questions for you and your fellow community members:

- What are the most important next-steps you need to take to leverage social media in your organization?
- What have been your greatest challenges in achieving adoption of social media?
- What wisdom have you gained during your experience?

7

LOOKING TO THE FUTURE

The reporter was due to arrive in twenty minutes, and the doctors were assembling in the conference room. WellCare's hospital administrator pulled on her jacket and reviewed her notes as she walked briskly down the hall. It had been quite a year for them. WellCare had been selected as a model hospital—profitable and efficient, with the best physicians on staff, and the ability to find solutions to the most difficult maladies suffered by its patients. Although businesses, government, and community organizations had been using social media over the past decade, the medical team felt that WellCare's adoption of social media tools was the critical factor in its ongoing success. Team members had used social media technology to centralize patient information, train new physicians, collaborate to treat patients, greatly improve patient care, and share their knowledge with the broader community. Most important, they were noted for their success rate in solving the most difficult and challenging patient cases.

The administrator remembered the early days of social media in the medical community. Back in 2009, the big news splash was how Detroit's Ford Hospital used YouTube and Twitter to share live surgeries with med students. Since then, this had become common practice, especially in the training hospitals. The medical community had found many more uses for social media, and her hospital was ahead of most others. Accuracy and efficiency were key priorities. For example, all medical records were electronically stored in a centralized and robust database, and a software application called Patient Profile served up the information to meet the needs of a variety of users. WellCare's physicians were equipped with wireless mobile devices that used voice recognition to enter all doctors' notes into the electronic file. Every device in the hospital transmitted data directly to the patient's file, noting temperature, weight, blood pressure, lab results, and X-ray images. Born from the design of the original social networking profiles, the Virtual File contains all patient history and does not sit in an office filing cabinet. Instead, the Virtual File resides on the Web and is available to anyone with proper access rights. Patients who are traveling can feel secure that any doctor across the globe will instantly know all their vital medical information and history.

Back at the hospital, the Patient Profile application has been instrumental in saving time, improving accuracy, and building an ecosystem of expertise to best treat the patient. As each specialist enters the room to work with the patient, his identification is automatically scanned, and his data and analysis are automatically captured in the correct fields in the system. Privacy controls have improved. With different access rights, family members can read the latest physician's diagnosis, notes, and treatment plans. As part of the patient ecosystem, the family members can add to the patient profile by describing changes they see in their loved one's condition. Keywords from any physician or family member and threshold metrics on vital signs automatically send a microblog to the patient's primary physician, alerting her to a significant change in condition. Even after the patient leaves the hospital, electronic monitors continue to add data to the patient's profile wirelessly, and threshold metrics trigger a microblog alert to the doctor. Patient blogs are scanned for keywords, and the doctor can comment on them, providing revisions to treatment plans or issuing new prescriptions that are ordered automatically with the pharmacy.

One of the biggest changes in physician behavior has been the extensive data mining and collaboration in which all physicians now engage. When stumped about a particular patient's case, each doctor can enter key symptoms into the patient profile research page. Any other cases with those symptoms come forward to the doctors (while identities are concealed). All a physician's notes are available as well as medications and treatment plans. In addition to patient profiles, extensive physician profiles are available in a vast social networking utility where they can discuss common challenges and innovative solutions. A discussion forum and microblogging capability enable physicians across the globe to consult with each other on their cases. The results have been stunning. Before, successful treatment plans were known only to those involved with the particular patient. Now those cases can be instantly shared with the people who need them, no matter where they are or who they "know."

Each week, specialists, pharmaceutical representatives, researchers, and selected patients convene in a virtual world to review their latest cases, share new experimental protocols, and discuss medication trials and side effects. Patient blogs and discussion forums are automatically scoured for specifically tagged data. These selected cases are shared as real-time patient samples, generating ideas in the community that might never before have been discovered. Through their collaboration and knowledge sharing, they speed the "breakthrough" process, and it is anticipated that cures for the most daunting diseases lie around the corner.

All these uses have enabled WellCare to become a hospital that has taken advantage of how social media improves its

ON THE HORIZON

internal operations and increases successful outcomes. The people at WellCare know there are many more uses for the tools they have now—just around the corner on the horizon. As she reached the conference room, the administrator made a note to herself: "Put out forum question to administrator network—what are the latest ways they use social media to work with patient advocates?"

The scenario we've glimpsed here is a fictitious example set in the future ... but the not-too-distant distant future. In fact, much of what we have described exists today. In Chapter Five, we discussed the Henry Ford Hospital's use of Twitter to educate medical students with a live surgery feed. At Rhön-Klinikum AG, a network of hospitals and clinics in Germany, electronic files are already shared among its network, and many health care organizations are currently automating their patient files.[1] Also, physicians are discovering the value of social networking sites such as Ozmosis and Sermo, specifically targeted to physicians, enabling them to share knowledge and to learn from each other.[2]

Perhaps the key differences in our slightly futuristic scenario rest in the "smart" search technology and in the mind-set of all involved. Those who possess this mind-set do not question the usefulness of new social media tools. Everyone recognizes that patients have valuable information to contribute and expect to input into the process. The notion of an ecosystem—a much broader one than we might use today—is prevalent, and this mind-set is fundamental to leveraging the collective knowledge that enables progress.

We are all on a Web-enabled journey to uncharted territory. The advent of social media technologies is changing the way we work in organizations and is having a direct impact on the bottom line. We've seen real examples of both for-profit and nonprofit organizations using social media to improve their performance.

These trailblazers are establishing a new way for organizations to achieve sustainable success. Although challenges exist, experimentation and lessons learned are giving these organizations a huge advantage over their competitors who still believe social media is just a passing fad. The advantages of social media for organizations are still emerging. So far, we've seen them add value most pervasively in the areas of attracting and retaining the best employees, talent development, operational efficiency, innovation, and knowledge creation.

Yet, savvy organizations are aware of their current environment and anticipate the environment of the future. Such understanding is essential to informing their strategic decisions. They cannot overlook the complexities and workforce dynamics of the changing landscape. Nor can they ignore the way people are now communicating and accomplishing work. Although not all organizations will embrace and support social media, increasingly more employees are insisting that the tools they use outside the workplace are enabled within the firewalls of the office, whether physical or mobile.

Companies like salesforce.com or Intel know the value of using microblogging and social networking sites to source the best candidates and show they have an organization that uses these tools freely. And Dow is tapping the wisdom of all generations in its workforce, from new hires to retirees. The arenas of human resources and organization development offers huge opportunities, such as talent management, the targeted identification of skills, succession planning, and mentoring through the use of robust social networking profiles. Oracle showed us that the learning process can be greatly improved by extending learning through communities and learner-generated content on blogs and forums. Given tools to gain efficiencies, people will naturally streamline their processes. We saw how Emergent Solutions accelerated its internal account management process as well as its customer responsiveness. But the company emphasizes that cocreation is its vision, and that's where organizations are really seeing the advantage of innovation and knowledge creation. BT's BTPedia is just one example of a way that employees generate and capture useful knowledge in the organization. In an ever-changing business environment, remaining competitive will require businesses to adapt to circumstances by fostering a strong commitment to innovation and leading-edge technologies. Social technologies can enable organizations to bring innovations to fruition much faster. To do so, members of the organization must be encouraged to actively contribute, and keeping them engaged over the long run will become essential.

The long-term advantage of creating a culture of engagement is clear. Social media plays to the heart of employees' engagement by providing a conduit for their contributions. As we've seen, while the future workforce evolves, an organization's industry advantage will depend largely on keeping employees engaged and connected.[3] Social networking sites may serve as a bridge that spans different cultures and fosters acknowledgment and understanding of diverse beliefs, practices, products, and services.

Despite the cynics who have reported the demise of the good old-fashioned handshake, building strong relationships is still fundamental in every kind of organization, and social media tools simply facilitate relationships between people that might not otherwise have an opportunity to interact. Over a decade ago, Kevin Kelly noted that "the central economic imperative of the network economy is to amplify relationships. Every aspect of a networked firm—from its hardware to its distributed organization—is created to increase the quantity and quality of economic relationships. The network is a structure to generate relationships."[4]

Today's trailblazers will soon be seen as the wise sages of social media's power within organizations. They understand that successful adoption of these tools and behaviors involves attention to both the process and the practice of implementation. These trailblazers continue to gather wisdom about how to ease the adoption of these tools, yet they recognize the challenges that lie ahead.

One challenge is that it will become increasingly difficult to retain proprietary knowledge, even with requirements for nondisclosure agreements. Another challenge will be for organizations to provide the means for employees to have candid conversations. Providing an environment that is safe, secure, and trusted will allow for those conversations to be of tremendous value not only to the individuals but also collectively to the organization that puts them to good use.[5]

The technology providers and members of the organization will become much more intelligent about how to protect personal privacy and corporate intellectual property. However, we believe the greater challenge to overcome will be people's resistance to this new paradigm. Like healthy organisms, healthy organizations thrive on adaptation—learning and adjusting. Will organizations be able to adopt new norms quickly enough to embrace social media use before the competition steals significant market share? Effective practices are still emerging in this new landscape, and you are part of the new collective wisdom being created every day.

How Changing Organizations Will Continue to Use Social Media

Time is marching by quickly, and the future arrives every day. As organizations continue to evolve, they will increasingly draw on the value of social media. Here are just a few of the ways we see organizations expanding their mind-set and their use of social media to help meet challenges on the horizon.

• *Social media will become a table stake.* Using Web 2.0 today is perceived as an organizational differentiator. A few organizations at the vanguard of social media are currently creating uniqueness by using it. Yet over the next decade or so, we envision social media becoming fundamental to every organization and will be "ante" for simply staying in the game. In the sea of potential sameness, what will differentiate social media users? We believe that actually deploying and using social media more effectively will become a key differentiator. Rather than simply sponsoring the technology, organizations will need to integrate social media for ongoing sustainability. In other words, as information content becomes pervasive, so will the demand for wisdom in harnessing and applying it. While conducting our research, we witnessed this phenomenon bubbling up all around us. Nevertheless, as its significance increases, good content may become even harder to discern. Skill in doing so can be an organization's secret weapon for success. In short, uniqueness will be defined by how well social media is aligned with and integrated into an organization's operational tapestry.

• *Trailblazers will become models for the envious who follow.* As trailblazers' performance improves and their stories are shared, other organizations will feel the irresistible pull to incorporate social media into their operations. Consequently, many more organizations will find their way through the pioneering and exploration phases, arriving at the leveraging phase, when they will derive exponential value from their use of social media. They will see these tools as more than just a conduit for communications. To truly capitalize on the connections occurring, organizations will work to integrate various communities and tools into a central Web space, as Intel is doing. In some cases, dedicated individuals or teams may be required to ensure that these tools and processes are embedded into all parts of the organizational system—gardeners on a grand scale.

• *Social media will play an increasing role in tapping the power of diversity.* The average age of the workforce will shift dramatically as more Millennials enter organizations and more Boomers exit with the company history under their arms. As this happens, the continuity of business will be at risk. Yet organizations can retain the knowledge and wisdom of current employees as well as alumni and retirees. With social media, conversations with retiring employees can be preserved in digital format and used to preserve organizational memory. Further, more retirees and alumni will remain engaged with their previous organizations through the many social media avenues available.

In a world in which work is executed around the clock, social media technologies will enable productivity across distances, languages, and time zones. They will become a primary tool for working virtually, resulting in real short-term and long-term impact as travel costs and "road warrior" fatigue are dramatically reduced.

Another trend resulting from globalization is the increasing number of mergers and acquisitions. Social media technologies can play a key role in speeding up company integration and the coalescing of corporate cultures and values. Because these tools enable open communication and the opportunity to tap ideas from any individual in the organization, the value of the human capital from acquired companies will be unleashed.

• *Organizations will become courageous enough to "let go."* As career life cycles morph, organizations of all kinds will have to make way for their members to enter and exit more easily. Contract workers, temporary assignments, and consulting engagements will become more commonplace. Corporate enterprises will have to let go of long-held beliefs about the traditional eight-hour day. They will also have to depart with past assumptions about communication flows and organizational structures. Outside of corporate environments, online communities can be "engineered" by design, or they can develop spontaneously and grow organically. Organizations can choose to engineer interest groups, but they will find it challenging to stop the spread of organic connections. Social media enables organizations to connect more closely with staff members *and* with customers and partners. Letting go of the perceived control of organizational communication can indeed be more advantageous in harnessing even more information—information that can be transformed into knowledge useful for competitive advantage. Indeed, in a McKinsey study, researchers were surprised at how much information flows through informal social networks and how little through formal hierarchical matrixes: "[I]t's unfortunate, at a time when the ability to create value increasingly depends on the ideas and intangibles of talented workers, that corporate leaders don't do far more to harness the power of informal networks."[6]

When decision makers loosen their grip, the natural communication flow will bring more intelligence to their fingertips. Leaders and teams will come to expect information anytime, anywhere, in any way that suits them. As they "get it," they will make more informed decisions, take greater risks, and shift priorities (and resources) more swiftly than in the past.

As we share more through social media, work will become increasingly more humane and more democratized. Social media will also change the very nature of the silent personal-organizational "contract" through which traditional organizations have held the power. As people gain more influence in the relationship, organizations will be forced to adopt less hierarchical structures and more egalitarian practices.

• *Shared knowledge will become a new currency*. Key challenges will arise as the shelf life of knowledge becomes shorter and shorter. For most organizations, the assumption is that key knowledge resides in the heads of a critical few individuals or teams. The advent of social media challenges this paradigm. In the future, more and more individuals and teams will be true contributors to the organization's proprietary intellectual property. Organizations can use the valuable knowledge to their competitive advantage.

Social technologies serve as a "marketplace" for the exchange of information. In this market, the key medium of exchange is knowledge, and the "wealthiest" traders are those organizations that are using the knowledge to improve their products and service offerings. Social technologies enable multiple simultaneous connections between groups of people, so that the potential value of the network is not just $n + n$, but n^n.[7] By capitalizing on these connections and linkages in a virtual trading marketplace, organizations can combine in multiple ways the various insights provided by thought leaders.

- *Social media will facilitate participation in a broader community.* Formal organizational boundaries will continue to blur, and new ones will become more defined by the organization's sense of community, rather than by its formal legal structures. In the blurring of boundaries, we will all more clearly see that we are each other's customers. Organizations will begin to realize that totally separating the internal from the external is a false dichotomy. In other words, one cannot divorce the internal from the external because internal uses and applications can drive external results, and vice versa. A common misconception is that an "organization" is a formal legal entity (a corporation, a nonprofit, a government body). As discussed throughout this book, many in the field of organization development tend to take a broader view of organizations as (sociotechnical) *systems.* We've advocated here for systems that are more open rather than closed. The use of social media will help redefine traditional views of organizations not as closed systems but as open entities that participate in a larger ecosystem.

How Social Media Itself Will Change

We cannot foretell the future, but we do believe we can see around the bend. Organizations all over the world are beginning to integrate social media into everything they do, and this is changing the way large and small organizations accomplish their goals. The use of social media is the next catalyst for huge change. Consider the evolution of music from vinyl to cassette to 8-track to CD to downloadable tunes. With the arrival of each new tool, the music lover's behaviors and norms shifted. We anticipate that social media will yield the same transformational impact. In the very near future, we will witness a continuous launch of new forms of social media technologies. Their inherently collaborative nature and the availability of open source software will accelerate their improvement to meet the changing needs of users. Here are just a few of the ways we see social media tools evolving.

- ***The variety and availability of social media will continue to proliferate.*** Remember when cell phones hit the marketplace years ago? One size fit all. Today we see cell phones and digital recording media of every size, variety, color, and capacity. Over a short period of time, social media has proliferated in type, reach, and capacity. The options are abundant. We see this potpourri of options continuing to grow exponentially as creative, tech-savvy developers improve on existing tools and invent solutions that meet our every need. Our thirst for helpful conveniences will keep the innovations coming in a continuous spiral. Just as "pervasive computing" spread in the late 1990s, social media will be everywhere, in both developed and developing countries, silently helping to transform our global socioeconomic landscape and redistributing social, financial, and intellectual capital. Social media will permeate everything we do—everywhere, all the time.

- ***Users will demand simplicity.*** The bubble-up process we described in Chapter Six is occurring globally, as organizations are embarking on the exploration phase, experimenting with a wide selection of tools to suit every need and preference. But individuals and organizations will eventually become overwhelmed with choice, and people will demand more integration. Rather than having to enlist multiple different social media tools to network or collaborate, people will begin to experience greater "aggregation" among disparate applications. Michael Arrington commented, "Now that there are services for virtually every kind of content that users might conceivably want to publish, we need open standards and businesses to emerge that help people link all their disconnected content together into a single online identity—the Centralized Me. This stuff is badly needed because our content is all over the place on the Internet."[8] The clarion call for simplicity will naturally force standards that will enable tools to be ubiquitous in all organizations. As users become more discerning and open source software becomes the norm, collectively we will formulate a few best-of-breed solutions and enter the leveraging phase. Globally, we will hum. This stage will be fleeting, however, as new technology and new work norms herald the next era of human connection.

In the meantime, individuals and organizations will reach a point where they will demand that their tools be both simple and smart. Simplicity in use and functionality will help maintain user sanity and allay a potential revolt. For example, a single core profile for each individual could be housed in a single place. From that profile, individuals would be able to tailor information for their various social networking communities, but the use of a consistent format for core information will greatly reduce the duplication that currently consumes needless energy. Jason Falls, cofounder of the Social Media Club of Louisville, Kentucky, shared this perspective on his blog: "Simplicity is the single thing people really want.... Fundamentally, removing the complexity and adding simplicity so you can easily access in an open way everything you want, and leverage a lot of social connections rather than going to multiple ones, is how the user experience will evolve."[9]

• *Social media tools will get smarter.* We all know that we live in the world of Web 2.0; each of us can create content and share it freely with others on the Internet. We can create Web pages, search for information, connect with others, and make online content accessible through multiple devices. This is the social media world of today; it is alive in the here and now. But Web 3.0 is rapidly emerging on the scene, adding increasing intelligence. We will enter the era of the "intelligence Internet" or the "semantic Web." Translation: "very smart stuff!" Whereas Web 2.0 enabled anyone to make connections through social media, Web 3.0 will facilitate smarter and more relevant connections. Intelligence will become embedded into social media tools so that we "connect with context." In other words, our connections will become richer and our social networking experiences more *meaningful*.

There is no shortage of information on any topic of choice. The new goal will be to *manage* the information so that it is most useful. Marshall Kirkpatrick, VP of content development at ReadWriteWeb, put it this way: "If Web 2.0 was all about democratizing publishing, then the next stage of the web may well be based on democratizing data mining of all that content that's getting published."[10] For example, new social media tools will be able to filter information to meet your requirements; they will analyze meaning, scan the Web, and serve up only content that is relevant to you (like a very smart RSS feed). We glimpsed at the value of smart tools in our futuristic hospital scenario.

What does Web 3.0 mean for organizations? They will be able to "mine" for data to find exactly the information that meets their needs. In every organization, data are precious business assets. With *smart* data, your employees can create knowledge that will become competitive, affecting the way they work, collaborate, and execute. With this increasing sophistication, learning within enterprises can truly accelerate. A savvy generation of collaborators will be able to cocreate what Peter Senge called the true "learning organization."[11]

- *Social media will continue to be viewed as both "good" and "bad."* Let's face it—social media is a controversial topic. We'd like to think that experimenting with social media always pans out, but there are definite risks. With increased use, dependency is inevitable. In April 2009, a clandestine team of troublemakers systematically cut AT&T fiber optic cables, creating a massive service outage in two Northern California cities.[12] Work in both cities halted—no Internet, no cell phone service, and no cable television for the entire population. Dubbed "cable crooks" and "fiber felons," these savvy saboteurs highlighted just how vulnerable we have become to technology failures. In addition, the value of transparency will continue to clash with the demands of privacy and security. It's almost schizophrenic. While demanding increasing visibility and accountability, many will resent how social media increasingly encroaches on their personal lives. In our work with a large credit union, some directors constantly complain about the inundation of meaningless, "non-value-added" chatter, while others complain about the lack of information and online participation. These dichotomies of perspective will always exist. As leaders and organizations, we will need to find new ways to constructively deal with the polarities.

How Society Will Use Social Media

We cannot resist the opportunity to think on a grander scale. We have seen how social media has expanded the ability of any organization to operate as a force across the globe to meet its goals. We anticipate that the way we define "organization" or "community" will expand as well to meet our collective global challenges. We see the broadening of "organizations" into global communities to solve the world's biggest challenges. Imagine the impact social media will have on the following world issues.

- *Social media will continue to shrink the global neighborhood.* The steam engine ushered commerce into a new era, linking trade and the transportation of goods to a larger marketplace.

When the airplane became a viable means of transportation for the general public, people began to travel more, and the world became smaller. In the same way, social media will become a way to make physical location a moot point in the formation of relationships. As people work more globally and make and maintain connections virtually, they will gain greater appreciation of diversity and culture.

- *Social media will change government.* We have already seen the seeds of this change in the United States. But for any government that seeks to serve the needs of its people, social media provides a ready means for constituents to have their voices heard. It will be inexcusable for elected officials not to understand the desires of those they represent.

- *Social media will boost the fitness of health care.* As we've seen in real case examples and in our imaginary scenario, social media has huge implications for the training of medical professionals and for operational efficiencies. In addition, the opportunities for collaboration among experts within a broader ecosystem will accelerate the identification of preventive measures and cures for the diseases that plague the planet. Researchers on the human genome project have already found that wikis are a valuable tool to promote collaboration and quality annotation. Imagine the possibilities for facilitating the collective genius of the biomedical and scientific communities.

- *Social media will take a bite out of crime.* Many reports cite the lack of coordination and collaboration among intelligence agencies and police forces. For example, regarding the tragic attack on the World Trade Center, the *9/11 Commission Report* noted that "the biggest impediment ... to a greater likelihood of connecting the dots—is the human or systemic resistance to sharing information."[13] Social media is all about sharing information. These tools can help foster a collaborative mind-set, transcending any natural resistance to coordinate efforts.

As law enforcement comes up to speed, victims themselves can leverage social media to ensure their own safety. In Atlanta, Georgia, citizens found each other on Facebook and formed a high-tech neighborhood watch program. Residents post surveillance videos on YouTube. Web-enabled cameras in their homes provide live, streaming video to the police department. Neighborhood watchdog groups armed with digital cameras and cell phones capture suspicious activity and instantly send their data to the authorities on Twitter and Facebook.[14] Similarly, Vasco Furtado, a professor at Brazil's Fortaleza University, created Wikicrimes, an application that links with Google Maps and enables citizens to share the location and details of crimes that take place in their neighborhoods.[15] Criminals beware.

- *Social media will facilitate social responsibility.* There are myriad ways that organizations as well as individuals will use social networking tools to come to each other's aid. One example is individual lending. Zopa.com is a social networking site specifically designed to connect borrowers with individual lenders. Rather than going directly to a bank, individual lenders select borrowers on the basis of the borrowers' personal stories and negotiated interest rates. Likewise, microlending is becoming more prevalent among those seeking worthwhile charities. Andy Finckle commented on a blog post that microcredit will increase because "People with money (PWM) will be 'closer' to people without money (PWOM)." Consequently, they will be better positioned to understand needs for microcredit, fund them, and receive instantaneous thanks through social media.[16]

- *Social media will help us band together across the globe.* Earthquakes, tsunamis, hurricanes, and other natural disasters disrupt global equilibrium. They have devastated entire regions, causing communities and nations to rally together in support across geopolitical boundaries. Less visible but perhaps more ominous, global warming threatens our very survival.

Underserved and underrepresented communities in developing nations are also clamoring for a voice on the stage of international affairs. No doubt, we are struggling to find solutions to unprecedented problems, and the use of social media can be an enabler of global collaboration.

The immensity of these problems necessitates the collective energy of every individual and organization, energy that can be harnessed and magnified through social media. As both natural and economic systems teeter on precarious ground, all the world's citizens must seek creative, lasting solutions that alleviate suffering and transform circumstances. From this macro view, the challenges are extraordinary, but so are the opportunities. We are organization development practitioners, not ecologists, politicians, or economists, but in our work with employees at all levels in global enterprises we see the collective capability found in organizations as a critical fulcrum in the greater global ecosystem. We are convinced that through social media, individuals in organizations—whether in large corporations, small entrepreneurial endeavors, or community networks—can contribute significantly, achieving more together than separately. None of us is as strong as all of us.

Begin the Journey

People have a natural need to connect, communicate, and collaborate with each other. The current Web 2.0 environment presents a huge opportunity for organizations of all kinds to meet this human need in a way that also promotes success for the organization. Social media at work is about how to exchange information and knowledge "just in time." It's not about the technology; it's about what people *do* with the technology. It's about exchange and a sense of community. It's about accessing valued information as needed and as desired. Social media technologies are much more than a fad; they will become a mainstream method of building competitive intelligence in organizations.

They enable organizations to "capitalize on connections" by giving their members a way to contribute to a common purpose. Strategies for using social media will continue to evolve. People make the network, and people are ingenious at finding ways to adapt technologies to meet their ever-changing needs.

We've discussed social media's impact on organizational performance, both today and in the near future. Social media in organizations is still virgin territory fraught with unknown opportunities and dangers. This path is not for the faint of heart. Yet for those who persist in embracing the adventure with both courage and tenacity, a world of innovative outcomes is the reward. We are confident that social media is here to stay, and when leveraged by the wise, can propel organizations to new levels of performance, competitiveness, and sustainability.

If your organization hasn't begun to use social media, we urge you to do so today! Find like-minded colleagues and capitalize on your connections. If yours has already embarked on this journey, stay the course, and mentor others along the way. The dividends are worth the investment—we know. In preparing this book, we conducted hundreds of interviews with individuals and organizations that have been and continue to be transformed by social media. The rewards have been greater than many ever imagined. We urge you, whoever and wherever you are, to begin to blaze your own trail, persist with gusto, and ultimately enhance your organization's vitality and success. Best wishes on your journey.

Join the Conversation

We again invite you to join the conversation, as you may already have at other points in the book. Please check out the Web site at www.socialmediaatwork-connection.com. Add your comments and help us all discover the best ways to connect, communicate, and collaborate to propel organizational performance.

Notes

Chapter One

1. Bossidy, L., Charan, R., & Burck, C. (2002). *Execution: The discipline of getting things done.* New York: Crown Business.
2. This concept is also known as crowdsourcing or community-based design. See http://en.wikipedia.org/wiki/Crowdsourcing.

Chapter Two

1. Kelly, E. (2006). *Powerful times: Rising to the challenge of our uncertain world.* Upper Saddle River, NJ: Wharton School Publishing.
2. Ford, H. (2003). *My life and work.* Whitefish, MT: Kessinger Publishing. (Original work published 1922)
3. Hanson, K. (2007). *Emerging elements of leadership in a complex system: A cognitivist approach.* Unpublished doctoral dissertation, University of San Diego, San Diego, California.
4. Davenport, T. (2009). Best practices for supporting knowledge workers. *CIO.* Retrieved May 1, 2009, from http://www.cio.com/article/29822/Best_Practices_for_Supporting_Knowledge_Workers?page=2.
5. Friedman, T. (2007). *The world is flat 3.0: A brief history of the twenty-first century.* New York: Picador, p. 10.

6. Dennis, V. (2009, Feb. 26). Nielsen report on most trafficked career sites. Cheezhead. Retrieved June 11, 2009, from http://www.cheezhead.com/2009/02/26/ved-nielsen-report-on-most-trafficked-career-sites/.

7. T. Bharwada (personal communication, April 20, 2009). Also see McDonald, D. *Is My Dow Network a social network?* Retrieved March 10, 2009, from http://www.ddmcd.com/my_dow.html.

8. Carpenter, J. (2009, March 30). Older workers searching for new jobs. Retrieved March 30, 2009, from http://www.cheezhead.com/2009/03/30/jc-older-workers-searching-for-jobs/.

9. Klink, S. V. (2008, May 14). *Corporate social networking* [Webinar]. SelectMinds.

10. U.S. Census Bureau, International Data Base. (n.d.). World population information. Retrieved March 29, 2009, from http://www.census.gov/ipc/www/idb/worldpopinfo.html.

11. Ibid.

12. Erickson, T. (2008). *Plugged in: The Generation Y guide to thriving at work.* Boston: Harvard Business School Press.

13. Ibid.
    Artley, J. B., & Mujtaba, B. *The art of mentoring diverse professionals.* Hallandale Beach, FL: Aglob Publishing, 2006.

14. Klink, S. V. (2008, May 14). *Corporate social networking* [Webinar]. SelectMinds.

15. Gordon, E. (2008). *Winning the global talent showdown.* San Francisco: Berrett-Koehler.
    Handy, C. (1998). *Beyond certainty: The changing world of organizations.* Boston: Harvard Business School Press.

16. Bateman, W. K., & Bateman, K. A. (2008). Jessica and Jason meet Maslow: Gen Y and the hierarchy of needs. In R. C. Preziosi (Ed.), *The 2008 Pfeiffer annual: Management development* (pp. 161–173). Hoboken, NJ: Wiley.

17. Artley, J. B., & Mujtaba, B. *The art of mentoring diverse professionals*. Hallandale Beach, FL: Aglob Publishing, 2006, p. 91.
18. Li, C., & Bernhoff, J. (2008). *Groundswell: Winning in a world transformed by social technologies*. Boston: Harvard Business Press.
    Pipl. (n.d.). 5 facts about social networking sites. Retrieved January 25, 2009, from http://pipl.com/statistics/ social-networks/5-facts/.
19. Fox Interactive. (2007, April). *Never ending friending*. Retrieved June 23, 2009, from http://creative.myspace .com/groups/_ms/nef/images/40161_nef_onlinebook.pdf.
20. Duncan, G. J., Boisjoly, J., & Harris, K. M. (2001). Sibling, peer, neighbor, and schoolmate correlations as indicators of the importance of context for adolescent development. *Demography, 38*, 437–448.
21. Business Wire. (2007, February 7). "Connection" and "collaboration" drive career choices for Generation Y workers, SelectMinds study finds. Retrieved June 11, 2009, from http://www.businesswire.com/portal/site/google/ ?ndmViewId=news_view&newsId=20070207005756 &newsLang=en.
22. Li, C., & Bernhoff, J. (2008). *Groundswell: Winning in a world transformed by social technologies*. Boston: Harvard Business School Press.
23. Datamonitor. (2007, October 24). World-wide social networking users by location. Cited on Will the Real Brad Baldwin Please Stand Up? Retrieved January 1, 2009, from   http://www.bradbaldwin.com/2007/10/24/world-wide -social-networking-users-by-location/.
24. Anderson, N. (2007, July 9). Report: South Korea tops in social networking, US fifth. Ars technica. Retrieved January 1, 2009, from http://arstechnica.com/news.ars/post/

20070709-report-south-korea-tops-in-social-network-us
-fifth.html.

25. Datamonitor. (2007). World-wide social networking users by location. Cited on Will the Real Brad Baldwin Please Stand Up? Retrieved January 1, 2009, from http://www.bradbaldwin.com/2007/10/24/world-wide-social-networking-users-by-location/.

26. JSRCC Library Blog. (2007, November). Social networking: Opinions and practices of library users and librarians. Retrieved February 2, 2009, from http://jsrcclibrary.wordpress.com/2007/11/.

27. Jacobs Media. (2007, April 11). Rockers of all ages use social networking sites. Retrieved June 23, 2009, from http://www.jacobsmedia.com/tech3_socnet.htm.
See Rapleaf. (2008, June 18). Rapleaf study of social network users vs. age. Retrieved January 1, 2009, from http://business.rapleaf.com/company_press_2008_06_18.html.
Rapleaf. (2008, July 29). Rapleaf study reveals gender and age data of social network users. Retrieved January 1, 2009, from http://business.rapleaf.com/company_press_2008_07_29.html.

28. Consumer Internet Barometer. (2008, June 13). Press release: Social networking takes off. Retrieved January 1, 2009, from http://www.consumerinternetbarometer.us/press.cfm?press_id=3413.

29. Wood, M. (2005, June 2). Five reasons social networking doesn't work. CNET. Retrieved January 1, 2009, from http://www.cnet.com/4520-6033_1-6240543-1.html.

30. comScore. (2008, August). Social networking explodes worldwide as sites increase their focus on cultural relevance. Retrieved June 25, 2009, from http://www.comscore.com/Press_Events/Press_Releases/2008/08/Social_Networking_World_Wide.

31. Li, C., & Bernhoff, J. (2008). *Groundswell: Winning in a world transformed by social technologies.* Boston: Harvard Business School Press.

32. MacManus, R. (2008, September 15). Report: Nearly 70% of businesses allow social media usage. ReadWriteWeb. Retrieved June 11, 2009, from http://www.readwriteweb.com/archives/report_businesses_social_media_usage.php.

33. Klink, S. V. (2008, May 14). *Corporate social networking* [Webinar]. SelectMinds.

34. McDonald, D. (2009). Is My Dow Network a social network? Retrieved January 1, 2009, from http://www.ddmcd.com/my_dow.html.

35. Havenstein, H. Dow launches social networking project. August 15, 2007. *Computerworld Networking and Internet.* Retrieved June 25, 2009, from http://www.computerworld.com/action/article.do?command=viewArticleBasic&articleId=9030719.

36. Klink, S. V. (2008, May 14). *Corporate social networking* [Webinar]. SelectMinds.

37. The Human Element Video. Retrieved January 15, 2009, from http://www.dow.com/careers/video/index.htm.

Chapter Three

1. J. Mulkey & G. Pope (personal communication, January 14, 2009).

2. Apollo Media Blog. (2008, June 9). The history of social media—Part 1. Retrieved April 10, 2009, from http://www.apollomediablog.com/a-brief-history-of-social-media-part-1/.

3. Li, C., & Bernhoff, J. (2008). *Groundswell: Winning in a world transformed by social technologies.* Boston: Harvard Business School Press.

4. Wikipedia. (n.d.). Wiki. Retrieved December 8, 2009, from http://en.wikipedia.org/wiki/Wiki.

5. Ibid.

6. Salzberg, S. (2007). Genome re-annotation: A wiki solution? PubMed Central. Retrieved February 12, 2009, from http://www.pubmedcentral.nih.gov/articlerender .fcgi?artid=1839116.

7. Police Act review wiki. (n.d.). Retrieved December 19, 2008, from http://www.policeact.govt.nz/wiki/.

8. Frishman, R., & Lublin, J. (2004). *Networking magic: Find the best—from doctors, lawyers, and accountants to homes, schools and jobs*. Avon, Mass.: Adams Media.

9. Rapleaf. (2008, June 18). Rapleaf study of social network users vs. age. Retrieved January 1, 2009, from http://www .rapleaf.com/company_press_2008_06_18.html.

10. Ibid.

11. Marketing Charts. (n.d.). Top 10 social-network, blog, web brand rankings issued for Dec [compiled by Nielsen]. Retrieved June 23, 2009, from http://images.google .com/imgres?imgurl=http://www.marketingcharts .com/wp/wp-content/uploads/2008/01/nielsen-online-top -10-social-networking-sites-us-december.jpg&imgrefurl= http://www.marketingcharts.com/interactive/top-10 -us-social-network-blog-web-brand-rankings-issued-for -dec-3097/nielsen-online-top-10-social-networking-sites -us-decemberjpg/&usg= ___qlmHwOt9OViB4766w7fI5zedIq8=&h=302&w=585 &sz=59&hl=en&start=6&um=1&tbnid= chPFKejfw9ydOM:&tbnh=70&tbnw=135&prev=/images %3Fq%3Dsocial%2Bneteworking%2Btop%2B10 %2Bnielsen%2B2009%26hl%3Den%26rls%3Dcom .microsoft:en-US%26rlz%3D1I7GGIT_en%26sa%3DN %26um%3D1.

12. Fahncke, M. (2008, May 30). *Social networking for authors* [Webinar sponsored by Stephaniegunning.com].

13. Womack, B. (2008, November). Twitter shuns venture-capital money as startup values plunge. Retrieved June 25, 2009, from http://www.bloomberg.com/apps/news?pid=20601109&sid=afu06n0L7LZ4.

Twitter.com. (2009). Hey there! Schwarzenegger is using Twitter. Retrieved June 25, 2009, from http://twitter.com/Schwarzenegger.

14. Steinberg, D. (2008, June). Zappos finds a user for Twitter. Really! Inc. Retrieved January 2, 2009 from http://www.inc.com/articles/2008/06/zappos.html.

15. Baker, S. (2008, May). Big Blue embraces social media. *BusinessWeek*. Retrieved June 6, 2009, from http://www.businessweek.com/magazine/content/08_22/b4086056643442.htm.

16. Virtual World Watch. (n.d.). Virtual worlds in UK higher and further education. Retrieved June 22, 2009, from http://virtualworldwatch.net/about/.

17. Stroud, J. (2009, January 27). Top 50 recruiters on Twitter. The Recruiter's Lounge. Retrieved June 23, 2009, from http://www.therecruiterslounge.com/2009/01/27/top-50-recruiters-on-twitter/.

Chapter Four

1. Corporate Leadership Council. (2004). *Driving employee performance and retention through engagement: A quantitative analysis of the effectiveness of employee engagement strategies.* Washington, DC: Corporate Leadership Council.

Gartland, M. P., & Shelton, C. D. (August, 2006). *Impact of organizational culture and person-organization fit on job satisfaction and commitment.* Paper presented at the annual meeting of the Academy of Management, Atlanta, GA.

2. Udechukwu, I. I., & Mujtaba, B. (2006). Employee turnover and social affiliation. In B. Mujtaba (Ed.), *The Art of Mentoring Diverse Professionals* (pp. 195–206). Hallandale Beach, FL: Aglob Publishing.

3. Orr, D., & Matthews, H. (2008). Employee engagement and OD strategies. *OD Practitioner, 40*(2), 18–23.

4. Human Capital Institute. (2008, Dec. 2). *Capturing the hearts and minds of young talent through blogs* [Webinar with Brazen Careerist].

5. Gold, P. (2009, March 12). Twittercruit: Should you use Twitter for recruiting? Social Workplace Blog, hire Strategies Ltd. Retrieved March 20, 2009, from http://blog .hirestrategies.co.uk/erecruitment/2009/03/twittercruit -should-you-use-twitter-for-recruiting.html.

6. Klink, S. V. (2008, May 14). *Corporate social networking* [Webinar]. SelectMinds.

7. Willis, T. J. (2008). *An evaluation of the technology acceptance model as a means of understanding online social networking behavior*. Doctoral dissertation, University of South Florida. Dissertation Information Service (UMI No. 3326103).

8. Web 2.0 in the workplace increases efficiency, but distractions, leaks a concern, say Europeans. (2008, November 12). Government Technology. Retrieved January 11, 2009, from http://www.govtech.com/gt/articles/558689?utm_source= rss&utm_medium=link.

9. Surowiecki, J. (2005). *The wisdom of crowds*. New York: Anchor Publishing, p. 10.

10. Owen, H. (2008). *Wave rider: Leadership for high performance in a self-organizing world*. San Francisco: Berrett-Koehler.

11. Web 2.0 in the workplace increases efficiency, but distractions, leaks a concern, say Europeans. (2008, November 12). Retrieved January 11, 2009, from http://www.govtech.com/ gt/articles/558689?utm_source=rss&utm_medium=link.

12. Klink, S. V. (2008, May 14). *Corporate social networking* [Webinar]. SelectMinds.

13. McKinsey & Company. (2008, July). Building the Web 2.0 enterprise. *McKinsey Quarterly*. Retrieved January 31, 2009,

from http://www.mckinseyquarterly.com/Building_the_Web_ 20_Enterprise_McKinsey_Global_Survey_2174.

14. International Quality and Performance Center. (n.d.). Social media for talent management [Brochure for the Social Media in Learning conference]. Retrieved April 2, 2009, from http://www.iqpc.com/uploadedfiles/EventRedesign/USA/ 2009/June/17310001/assets/brochure.pdf.

15. Tapscott, D., & Williams, A. D. (2006). *Wikinomics: How mass collaboration changes everything.* New York: Portfolio, p. 18.

Chapter Five

1. Walker, J. (2008, June 23). Salesforce.com goes Web 2.0 recruiting. Recruit the Web 2.0 Way. Retrieved June 11, 2009, from http://john-walker.info/recruitment -technology/salesforcecom-does-web-20-recruiting/.

2. Marte, J. (2009, Jan. 4). Twitter yourself a job. *Wall Street Journal.* Retrieved June 11, 2009, from http://online .wsj.com/article/SB123103484826451655.html?mod= googlenews_wsj.

3. Taylor, M. (2009, January 29). The Pope embraces YouTube, Facebook. *Wall Street Journal* [Blogs]. Retrieved June 11, 2009, from http://blogs.wsj.com/digits/2009/01/29/ the-pope-embraces-youtube-facebook/.

4. Wenger, E., McDermott, R., & Snyder, W. M. (2002). *Cultivating communities of practice: A guide to managing knowledge.* Boston: Harvard Business School Publishing.

5. Tapscott, D., & Williams, A. D. (2008). *Wikinomics: How mass collaboration changes everything.* New York: Penguin Group, p. 240.

6. UgoTrade. (2008, June 16). Philips Design's ideation quest in Second Life. Retrieved June 11, 2009, from http://www .ugotrade.com/2008/06/16/philips-designs-ideation-quest -in-second-life.

7. McGirt, E. (2009, March 17). How Chris Hughes helped launch Facebook and the Barack Obama campaign. *Fast Company*. Retrieved June 26, 2009, from http://www.fastcompany.com/magazine/134/boy-wonder.html.

8. Stirland, S. L. (2008, May 19). Democrats launch McCainpedia, an attack site masquerading as a wiki. *Wired*. Retrieved June 11, 2009, from http://www.wired.com/threatlevel/2008/05/democrats-launc/.

9. Carr, D. (2008, November 10). How Obama tapped into social networks' power. *New York Times*. Retrieved June 11, 2009, from http://www.nytimes.com/2008/11/10/business/media/10carr.html.

10. LaMonica, M. (2006). IBM warms to social networking. *ZDNet News*. Retrieved January 28, 2009, from http://news.zdnet.com/2100-3513_22-149740.html.

11. Faust, J. E. (1999, May). *Ensign*, pp. 18–19. Retrieved June 22, 2009, from http://tech.lds.org/index.php?option=com_content&view=article&id=199&Itemid=6.

12. Brzozowski, M. J. (2009). WaterCooler: Exploring an organization through enterprise social media. In *Proceedings of the 2009 international conference on supporting group work*. May 10–13, 2009, Sanibel Island, Florida, USA. ACM Press.

13. Ibid., pg. 7.

14. Maihack, B. (July, 2008). Personal communication. Ceguerra, L. (2009). Personal communication.

15. Pinto, B. (2009, March 22). Using Twitter to teach: Surgeons 'tweet' from operating room during brain surgery. *ABC News*. Retrieved June 11, 2009, from http://abcnews.go.com/GMA/Weekend/story?id=7140272&page=1.

16. Ibid.

17. L. Chen & G. Brower (personal communication, February 2, 2009).

18. Watkin, C., & Hubbard, B. (November, 2003). Leadership motivation and the drivers of share price: The business case

for measuring organizational climate. *Leadership & Organizational Development Journal, 24*(7), 380–386.

Whelan-Berry, K. S. (2006). *Did the organizational culture really change? Show me the data.* Salt Lake City, UT: Utah Valley State College (presented at the 2006 Academy of Management Annual Meeting, Atlanta, GA).

Gartland, M. P. (2006). *Impact of organizational culture and personal-organizational fit on job satisfaction and commitment.* Kansas City, MO: Rockhurst University (point paper presented at the 2006 Academy of Management Annual Meeting, Atlanta, GA).

19. Adler, P. S., & Kwon, S. W. (2002). Social capital: Prospects for a new concept. *Academy of Management Review, 27*(1), 17–40.

20. Tapscott, D., & Williams, A. D. (2008). *Wikinomics: How mass collaboration changes everything.* New York: Penguin Group, pp. 224–245.

21. Howlett, D. (2007). The social network penny drops at Oracle. ZDNet. Retrieved June 11, 2009, from http://blogs.zdnet.com/Howlett/?p=122.

22. IBM. (2009). *IBM virtual onboarding with Second Life* [YouTube video]. Retrieved June 11, 2009, from http://www.youtube.com/watch?v=s21YDrBm9F4.

23. IBM. (2009). Overview of Beehive. Retrieved June 25, 2009, from http://domino.watson.ibm.com/cambridge/research.nsf/0/8b6d4cd68fc12b52852573d1005cc0fc?OpenDocument.

Intranet Insider. (2009). Beehive builds buzz at IBM. Retrieved June 25, 2009, from http://www.communitelligence.com/blps/blg_viewart.cfm?bid=59&artID=551.

24. Klink, S. V. (2008, May 14). *Corporate social networking* [Webinar]. SelectMinds.

25. Hanwell, M. (2009, Mar. 4). Personal communication.

26. Forsberg, A., & Komonen, J. (2008, October). *Renewing Nokia's culture and values: Web 2.0 to support change.* Paper presented at the annual conference of the OD Network, Austin, TX. Ian Gee and Antti Miettinen were part of the change management team that orchestrated the effort.

Chapter Six

1. A. Bacal & Associates. (2009). What is an environmental scan? Strategic and Business Planning Free Resource Center. Retrieved May 1, 2009, from http://www.work911 .com/planningmaster/faq/scan.htm.
2. Epicor. (n.d.). Bringing Web 2.0 to the enterprise: Leveraging social computing technologies for ERP applications. *CIO.* Retrieved April 12, 2009, from http://www.cio.com/documents/whitepapers/BringingWeb2.0.pdf.
3. Kaplan, R. S., & Norton, D. P. (2001). *The strategy-focused organization: How Balanced Scorecard companies thrive in the new business environment.* Boston: Harvard Business School Press.
4. Kaplan, R. S., & Norton, D. P. (2004). *Strategy maps: Converting intangible assets into tangible outcomes.* Boston: Harvard Business School Publishing.
5. Gladwell, M. (2002). *The tipping point.* New York: Back Bay Books.
6. Rapleaf. (2008). *Rapleaf study of social network users vs. age.* Retrieved January 1, 2009, from http://business.rapleaf.com/company_press_2008_06_18.html.
7. Heath, C., & Heath, D. (2007). *Made to stick: Why some ideas survive and others die.* New York: Random House, p. 13.
8. Ibid., p. 18.
9. Fahncke, M. (2008, May 30). *Social networking for authors* [Webinar sponsored by Stephaniegunning.com].
10. ThinkQuest Team 16325. (1998, August 31). Aztecs: Conquest. Retrieved June 11, 2009, from http://library .thinkquest.org/16325/y-conq.html.

11. Gerus, C. (Ed.). (2007). *Leadership moments: Turning points that changed lives and organizations*. Victoria, BC: Trafford, p. i.

Chapter Seven

1. Kleinshmidt, A. (2008, Fall). Electronic patient records. *Pictures of the Future*. Retrieved June 11, 2009, from http://a1 .siemens.com/innovation/en/publikationen/publications_ pof/pof_fall_2008/patientenakte.htm.
2. Mesko, B. (2008, April 11). *Ozmosis vs. Sermo: Answers*. Retrieved May 1, 2009 from http://scienceroll.com/ 2008/04/11/ozmosis-vs-sermo-answers/.
3. Benko, C., & Weisberg, A. (2007). *Mass career customization: Aligning the workplace with today's non-traditional workforce*. Boston: Harvard Business School Press.
4. Kelly, K. (1998). *New rules for the new economy: 10 radical strategies for a connected world*. New York: Viking Penguin.
5. Meister, J. C. (2008, April). Learning for the Google generation. *Chief Learning Officer*. Retrieved January 28, 2009, from http://www.clomedia.com/in-conclusion/jeanne -c-meister/2008/April/2142/index.php.
6. Bryan, L. L., Matson, E., & Weiss, L. M. (2007, November). Harnessing the power of informal networks: How formalizing a company's ad hoc peer groups can spur collaboration and unlock value. *McKinsey Quarterly*. Retrieved March 30, 2009, from http://www.mckinseyquarterly.com/ Harnessing_the_power_of_informal_employee_networks_ 2051.
7. Kelly, K. (1998). *New rules for the new economy: 10 radical strategies for a connected world*. New York: Viking Penguin.
8. Arrington, M. (2008, June 2). The future of social isn't content spewing (I hope). TechCrunch. Retrieved May 1, 2009, from http://www.techcrunch.com/2008/06/02/ the-future-of-social-isnt-content-spewing-i-hope/.
9. Falls, J. (2008, Dec. 3). Predicting the future of social media. Social Media Explorer. Retrieved May 1, 2009, from

http://www.socialmediaexplorer.com/2008/12/03/predicting
-the-future-of-social-media/.

10. Kirkpatrick, M. (2009, April 15). The future of social media monitoring. ReadWriteWeb. Retrieved May 1, 2009, from http://www.readwriteweb.com/archives/whats_next_in_ social_media_monitoring.php.

11. Senge, P. (1990). *The 5th discipline: The art and practice of the learning organization.* New York: Doubleday.

12. Asimov, N., Kim, R., & Fagan, K. (2009, April 10). Sabotage attacks knock out phone service. *SF Gate.* Retrieved May 1, 2009, from http://www.sfgate.com/cgi-bin/article .cgi?f=/c/a/2009/04/09/BAP816VTE6.DTL&tsp=1.

13. National Commission on Terrorist Attacks Upon the United States. (2004, July 22). *9/11 Commission Report.* Retrieved June 23, 2009, from http://www.9-11commission.gov/ report/911Report.pdf, p. 417.

14. ABC News. (2009, May 2). Neighborhood watch goes high tech. Retrieved May 2, 2009, from http://abcnews.go .com/search?searchtext=Atlanta%20neighborhood %20watch&type=.

15. eGovernment Resource Centre. (2008, November 13). Wikicrimes. *What's New Newsletter.* Retrieved May 1, 2009, from http://www.egov.vic.gov.au/index.php?env=-innews/ detail:m3097-1-1-8-s-0:n-1663-1-0--.

16. Finckle, A. (2008, August 28). The future of social media [Comment]. Global Neighbourhoods. Retrieved May 1, 2009, from http://redcouch.typepad.com/weblog/2008/08/ the-future-of-s.html.

Acknowledgments

When we conceived the idea to write this book, little did we anticipate the outpouring of enthusiasm and assistance that would be so generously offered to us, by experts and practitioners alike, from so many different corners of the social media world. The conversations have been magical, and we hope to continue these relationships for years to come. We are extremely grateful to the following individuals and companies for graciously allowing us to learn from and incorporate their experiences into this work.

First, we must thank the trailblazers we highlight in our case studies for their time in speaking with us about their insights and ideas, and for candidly sharing their experiences and lessons learned: Jamie Mulkey, Ed.D., and Greg Pope from the Association of Test Publishers; Richard Dennison from BT; Greg Brower and Linda Chen of Cisco; Trish Bharwada; Chris Cavanaugh-Simmons, Dave Ancel, and Dave Simpson of Emergent Solutions; Don Kraft, Ed.D., and Omar Nielsen of Genentech; Gino Creglia of Gino Creglia Photography; Lourdes Ceguerra and Brad Mahack of Hewlett-Packard; David Woodbury of Humana; Laurie Griffith Buczek and Steven Snyder of Intel; Andreas Forsberg, Johanna Komonen, and Matthew Hanwell of Nokia; and John Bansavich, Ed.D., and Ginny Wallace from the University of San Francisco.

We are fortunate to work at Oracle, an organization that values innovation and is constantly forging new ground to help organizations achieve their goals. We thank the following colleagues for sharing their experiences and examples: Jake

Kuramoto and Paul Pedrazzi from applications development; Mark Bennett and Amy Wilson from fusion product strategy; Patricia Cureton and Titina Ott from the Oracle Women's Leadership program (OWL); Mark Milani from the service engineering Global Leadership Academy. In addition, our thanks go to our global colleagues on the Global Organization and Talent Development (OTD) group and the human resources team for their courage in bringing social media to the learning and organization development efforts at Oracle. In particular we thank Kirsten Hanson, Ed.D., for her tremendous support, authenicity and receptivity to experimentation. A special thanks to Anje Dodson, vice president of human resources, for championing our mission in OTD; and to Joyce Westerdahl, senior vice president of human resources at Oracle, for her support.

Many people have informed our thinking. Although we couldn't possibly thank everyone who shared so generously with us, we'd like to acknowledge the following for their research, suggestions, and support: Mike Abrams of TBD Consulting; Virginia Brady of UFirst Federal Credit Union and Credit Union Executives Society; Marty Fahncke of FawnKey & Associates; Beryl Fajardo, Ed.D., and Sal Falleta, Ed.D., of Leadersphere; Dana Goodrow from TeenNow California; Kristen Harjo of Kraft; David Hinds of Hinds & Associates; Prasad Kaipa, Ph.D., of the Kaipa Group; Eugene Kim of Blue Oxen; Gaynor Lloyd-Davies of BT; Jill Lublin; Ross Mayfield of SocialText; Cheryl McDowell; Steve McMahon of SuccessFactors; Deborah Meehan and the Leadership Learning Community; Renee Moorefield of Wisdom Works; Amanda Noz; Sandy O'Gorman of ARC International; Harrison Owen of H. H. Owen and Company; Mital Poddar of Synopsis; Lauren Powers; Phil Quinn of Quinn Interactive; Greg Ranstrom; Ron Riggio of the Kravis Leadership Institute; Lorraine Rinker of Rinker & Associates; Scott Saslow and Nancy Thomas of the Institute of Executive Development; Rayona Sharpnack of the Institute for Women's Leadership; Bill Slingland of Talon Associates; Courtney Timmons, Blake Bush, Ben Katz, and Jack

Schaedler of Enspire; Denise Tittle and Mike Shoemaker of Personnel Decisions International; Chris Williams of Market Out Loud; Ken Williams of the AED Center for Leadership Development; and Jack Zenger of Zenger Folkman. Also, we want to acknowledge the many conversations and the collaborative energy at conferences and professional organizations where we enjoy membership: the Academy of Management, American Society for Training and Development, the Authors Guild, Coaches Training Institute, the Institute for Executive Development, International Leadership Association, Organization Development Network, and the Professional Business Women of California. We are particularly grateful to our early draft reviewers and endorsers for their responsiveness, feedback, and enthusiasm for this work.

Bringing a book to print is never as simple as it would seem. We are so appreciative of the excellent team at Jossey-Bass. Our editor, Genoveva Llosa, had tireless energy and patience in guiding us toward one cohesive direction. Her eagle eye and expertise were the keys to corralling our efforts. Gayle Mak, editorial assistant, kept us on track at all times and guided us through the treacherous waters of approvals and permissions. Michele Jones, our tenacious copy editor, worked her magic with words. Mark Karmendy, editorial production manager, put the glint in our eyes by making our words a tangible and beautiful product. Erin Moy, our marketing manager, helped get us in front of so many eyes and into your hands. Rob Brandt, editorial projects manager; Debbie Notkin, our contracts manager; and many others were helpful behind the scenes. We're especially grateful to Rebecca Browning, our initial acquisitions editor, for believing we had a great topic to share with readers and launching our journey.

And to our dear family and friends, a heartfelt thanks! To Mary Ellen's family—George, Yianni, and Sophia Kassotakis— our appreciation for their encouragement and patience. To her parents, John and Sophia Evrigenis, and her grandparents, special thanks and gratitude for the high value they placed as parents on education and lifelong learning. We are thankful to Jackie's husband, Jeff, for always supporting her passions and pursuits and for knowing to bring her dinner at the local coffeehouse. To Jackie's sister, Jan, sincere thanks for always reading each draft "one more time." And much gratitude to Jackie's friends Andrea and Lana for never getting tired of asking with genuine interest, "How's the book coming along?" To Arthur Jue's family—parents, Raymond and Nora, as well as siblings, Lorine, Daniel, and family—our tremendous gratitude for their unconditional support and assistance, and to the Neumillers—Bob, Corine, Amelia, and Grace—we give our heartfelt thanks for their ongoing inspiration and continuous empathy.

As collaborators, we've truly enjoyed the opportunity to connect, communicate, and create together. Despite the long nights, early mornings, difficult decisions, and diversity of perspectives, we would do it again in a heartbeat. To one and all, thank you for making this such a wonderful and unforgettable journey.

Arthur L. Jue
Jackie Alcalde Marr
Mary Ellen Kassotakis
September 2009

About the Authors

Arthur L. Jue, DM, MBA/TM, CCD, is a director of global organization and talent development for Oracle. He has extensive senior leadership experience in technology companies, such as IBM and Hyperion. He also serves on the board of directors for financial services, educational, and nonprofit organizations, such as the Boy Scouts of America Santa Clara County Council, SJSU Business Alumni Network, Meriwest Credit Union, Tongan Leadership Academy, and International Leadership Association.

Arthur holds a doctor of management in organizational leadership and an MBA with emphasis in technology management. He attended Brigham Young University and earned a BS in marketing with a music minor from San Jose State University. In addition, Arthur has participated in executive programs at the London Business School, Harvard University, and the University of Oxford. He is a member of Phi Kappa Phi and Beta Gamma Sigma, serves on the editorial board of the *Journal of Management, Spirituality, and Religion*, and is on the Academy of Management's MSR executive board.

Arthur's writing has been featured in such publications as the *Journal of Applied Management and Entrepreneurship*, *NHRD Network Journal*, and *Journal of Human Values*. He has also coauthored a number of books, including the *Pfeiffer Annual on Management Development*, *Leadership Moments: Turning Points That Changed Lives and Organizations*, and *Scholarship Pursuit: The*

How-To Guide for Winning College Scholarships. Arthur is a faculty member in the graduate schools of business for Northcentral University and the University of Phoenix. In addition, he is a member of the international faculty and advisory board of the Center for Leadership, Innovation, and Change at the Indian School of Business. Arthur has been a missionary in New Zealand, is an Eagle Scout, and enjoys playing the violin.

Jackie Alcalde Marr, MHROD, CPCC, is the director of organization and talent development for Oracle, North America. She has had more than twenty years of experience in the field of organization development with Fortune 100 companies. She has led leadership and professional development organizations, assisted leaders with talent management and strategic planning, and led change management consulting engagements for large information technology implementations. Jackie has worked with global leaders and teams throughout Europe, Latin America, and Asia. While living in England, she helped create a change management consulting practice for Oracle.

Jackie is an adjunct faculty member at the University of San Francisco, where she teaches organization development at both the undergraduate and graduate levels. She has presented at several national conferences and has been published in *Organization Development Journal* and *Sacramento Business* magazine. Jackie is the founder of Evolutions Consulting Group. She is a certified executive and personal coach and enjoys serving as a Sacramento Area Success Team Leader, helping community leaders and individuals clarify and achieve goals through planning, social networking, and coaching. She participates in the Organization Development Network, the American Society for Training & Development, the Sacramento Coaches Association, and the Social Media Club of Sacramento, and serves on the advisory committee for the Sacramento Professional Business Women of California.

Jackie holds a master's degree in human resources and organization development from the University of San Francisco and a bachelor's degree in psychology and communications with a minor in Spanish from California State University, Sacramento. She is certified in ODR's Managing Organizational Change, Pritchett's Change Management program, Buzan Centre's Mind Mapping, the Myers-Briggs Type Indicator, and the PDI 360 assessment. In addition, she has training in balanced scorecard and ROI strategies. Jackie resides in Folsom, California, with her husband, Jeff, and mischievous mutt, Guinness.

Mary Ellen Kassotakis, Ed.D., MBA, CPCC, CPT, is leader of the Leadership Center of Excellence within Oracle's Global Organization and Talent Development group. She has more than twenty years of experience in large, global companies; her areas of expertise include organization development, leadership development, strategic planning, diversity, coaching, and change management. Mary Ellen's academic background includes a doctorate in educational leadership from the University of Southern California, an MBA from San Francisco State University, and a B.A. from the University of California, Berkeley.

Mary Ellen is certified as a leadership coach and as a Human Performance Technologist. She is qualified to administer the following assessment tools: 360° Assessments (Personnel Decisions International, The Booth Company), the Myers-Briggs Type Indicator (MBTI®), Firo-B® Fundamental Interpersonal Relations Orientation-Behavior, and the Thomas-Kilmann Conflict Mode Instrument Profile and Interpretive Report. Additional training and specialized certifications and training include Extraordinary Leader as Coach (Zenger-Folkman), Flawless Consulting Skills (Designed Learning), Group Facilitation Skills (Community at Work), Applied Organization Development (Yarbrough & Associates), Successfully Executing

Strategic Change (Conner Partners), and Managing Transitions (William Bridges).

On the international scene, Mary Ellen is active with the International Leadership Association's Business Executive Committee, the Organization Development Network, and the International Coach Federation. In the greater Sacramento area, Mary Ellen volunteers with Shriners Hospitals for Children Northern California and is an advisor to the Sacramento Professional Business Women of California. She has worked with leaders of the Roseville Joint Unified High School District, Girl Scouts of Tierra del Oro, Families First, the Junior League of Sacramento, the National Charity League, as well as the local chapters of the American Society for Training & Development and the Sacramento Organization Development Network. When time permits, Mary Ellen is a recreational golfer.

Index